Gap Analysis

Using Archetypal Imprints to Bridge Staff Mindset Gaps

David J. Hulings
(with Dr. Lori Tubbergen Clark)

Gap Analysis

Using Archetypal Imprints to Bridge Staff Mindset Gaps

To my clients, you elevated our learning together!

Acknowledgments

As in prior material, this book would not have been possible if it weren't for the years of research, study and writings by Dr. Carol Pearson, Dr. Hugh Marr, and Dr. Kesstan Blandin. The Pearson-Marr Archetype Inventory (PMAI) ® has revolutionized the way the common man on the street learns and understands the interaction of their archetypal imprints and their daily journey. I would not have developed the thoughts and ideas in this book without their inspiration and valuable knowledge. Thank you!

Table of Contents

Acknowledgments

Foreword i

Author Biography - David iv

Author Biography - Lori v

Preface vi

    -Bill- vi

    -Julie- vii

    -Ken- viii

Introduction x

    Cognitive Anchors xi

    Assumed Constraints xv

    Your Personal Ochyroma xx

PART 1 Understanding how a Mindset is Formed 1

    Mindset – Muscle Memory 4

    Fixed or Fluid? Activities to Do (Will Power vs. Way Power) 5

    Transactional or Transformational? 7

    The Ever-Flowing Thought River of Life 8

    Beliefs > Values > Passions > Purpose (Commitments and/or Fears) 11

    Individualization 21

PART 2 Understanding How Our Archetypal Stories Impact and Express Our Mindset 24

PART 2a 12 Archetypes Described (The possible stories of our mindsets) 26

    Basic Archetype Understanding 26

    The Twelve Archetypes 31

    Ten Archetype Exercises 35

PART 2b 12 Archetypes Applied (The connection between mindset and your archetype story) . 57

PART 3 Renewing the Mind 72

Summary of Parts 1-3 96

PART 4 Best-fit strategies to organizational staffing **101**

Conclusion: The Power of Life's LEGO Blocks! **127**

Addendum A – David's Bucket List **129**

Addendum B – Each Archetype's Possible Ochyroma **130**

Addendum C – David's Life Laws **133**

Addendum D – Change Matrix **135**

Addendum E – Sample Stakeholder Survey Questions **138**

Addendum F – Archetype Team Profile Sample and Gap Analysis Processing Questions **139**

Addendum G - Archetypal Word Bank **141**

Addendum H - 6-Minute Screening Criteria **143**

Addendum I – Candidate Data Organizer **144**

Foreword

Curt Ellis, Assistant Superintendent, Human Resources
Saline Area Schools, Saline, MI

"Saline Area Schools has been engaged with David Hulings since 2008 to provide executive coaching for our administrative team. During the coaching sessions, David often provides our administrators with a deep and reflective "look in the mirror" using archetypes. This process not only provides our administrators with a clearer understanding of who they are and what motivates their behavior, it helps them peek inside the windows of their coworkers to better understand them as well. The ability to obtain a level of self-awareness, as well as an awareness of those we work with, has proven invaluable as we navigate the changes demanded of us!"

Scott E. Little, Associate Executive Director
Michigan School Business Officials, Lansing, MI

For many years, I have had the privilege of working with David Hulings as he coaches school professionals to become informed, effective, leaders. He's created tools that help everyone better understand how to utilize archetypes, while also preparing to better manage change in any environment. This book outlines and explains one of those tools he has provided our clients.

Scott Menzel, Superintendent
Scottsdale Unified School District, Scottsdale, AZ

In an environment where expectations are high, and there is no shortage of "solution providers", Hulings and Associates' coaching of staff stands apart from others by focusing on growing leaders through a journey of self-discovery that leads to purposeful and meaningful action based on a deep understanding of their archetypes. Misalignment between job expectations and a leader's internal wiring often leads to under performance and can ultimately result in loss of employment. For the leader who is willing to take the time to understand their archetypes, the dividends payoff in improved performance and enhanced job satisfaction. Having worked with Mr. Hulings for more than fifteen years across three separate school systems, I can attest to the power of the model and the positive impact on staff.

Denny Costerison, Executive Director
Indiana Association of School Business Officials Indianapolis, Indiana

David is a mentor, coach, and trusted friend who tackles various leadership styles and makes them understandable. His presentation style on archetypes is a positive guide to thoughtful decision-making, which assists the reader in evaluating their need for change. David articulates his change matrix in a way that opens windows that were not there before and creates transformational change for the reader.

William Heath
Superintendent, Portland Public Schools
Portland, MI

Throughout my career in the U.S. Navy and later in public education, I have had the opportunity to witness various leadership styles. One thing is always consistent: effective leadership and organizational management stem from a deep understanding of one's self and the people they work with. Without this self-awareness, nothing in our environment can truly change. David Hulings will show you the mirror of truth by guiding and coaching you on a significant journey that will help you to understand how your archetypes have been and continue to be influenced and how they influence others. The results will be a profound insight into yourself and those surrounding you. Knowledge is power, and knowing your people will give you the power to care for your team, create change, and reach new heights of success. David has been instrumental in my own journey. He has and continues to provide me with the tools to be a better leader and a better person.

Susan Harkin
Superintendent, Community Unit School District 300
Algonquin, IL

The use of archetype work with the District 300 leadership team has significantly impacted our work approach. Instead of viewing our team's differences as a disadvantage, we intentionally use them to strengthen our team. Whenever new members join our team, we assess their archetype to determine how their unique hardwiring will benefit our group. Using the archetype inventory, we can tap into our unique gifts and address any shadow traits hindering our team's progress. As a result of this work, we are better able to operate as a highly effective team to best serve our students.

Eric Hoppstock
Superintendent, Berrien Springs RESA
Berrien Springs, MI

If we are honest as leaders, it is difficult to get a group of people to pull in a singular direction to achieve outstanding outcomes. This is especially true if that group is made up of other leaders and you are a leadership group. Each leader brings unique traits and skills to the group that can advance the cause or become a significant distraction. Learning how to appreciate these traits, especially when they are very different than your own, and to maximize these to the greatest good is worth the effort.

To guide a group through the storm of change or put another way to challenge their own perception and tendencies toward a different way of behavior. To re-norm practices and tendencies that not only benefit the whole, but help the individual realize their own potential is worth the effort. To change a mindset to a better way of thinking is truly miraculous. This effort results in outstanding performance and, when blended into a group, allows a group of people to accomplish outstanding things that they did not think possible. This change is not easy, but the learning of archetypes and transformational changes in thinking can make all the difference.

Author Biography - David

Years ago, David was sent on a journey, but not of his own choosing or making. A broken marriage would end one career as a church pastor, but by God's grace, it would also open the door to another.

Executive leadership coaching was not on David's life plan, but thirty years later, after hundreds of one-on-one coaching sessions and thousands of hours of learning more, it has changed that life plan. Since that devastating turn in the road, David has not only crafted a successful leadership coaching business but has enjoyed every minute of it. Why? Because it has fulfilled the purpose of his life. Written on the wall of his office, it reads:

To be available, to provide tools, to equip leaders, to do good to the glory of my God.

David has been blessed with a passion for transforming the lives of those he meets, especially those who lead others. Hulings & Associates started out as a business but has turned into a calling. Along with some amazing associates, David looks to find a way to equip leaders to get from point A to point B. This is why he refers to himself as a leadership coach.

The etymology of coach is that of a buggy, which was created to take you from where you are to where you want to go. Whether he is speaking, writing books and/or training modules, designing individualized leadership tools, or conducting one-on-one coaching sessions, David's desire is to make sure clients and organizations archive their desired ends and reach their planned destinations.

When David is not engaged in transformation work, he enjoys life with his amazing wife, Robin May, along with their seven children and numerous grandchildren and great-grandchildren. Living on the west coast of Michigan, he loves traveling with Robin to their second home, Way Maker, their boat located on the west coast of Florida. To David, creativity begins on the water and ends up in his speaking and writing.

Author Biography - Lori

Lori Tubbergen Clark, educator, entrepreneur, public speaker, and culture champion, is delighted to join David Hulings in his latest work, Gap Analysis! Using Archetypal Imprints to Bridge Staff Mindset Gaps.

Hailing from Fremont, Michigan, Lori has a doctoral degree in Educational Leadership and Counseling from Eastern Michigan University, holds the Michigan Superintendent Specialist endorsement, and several certifications. She has served the education community as a teacher, consultant, executive administrator and school superintendent. After 35 years in educational leadership, Lori is currently an executive coach and consultant working with Hulings & Associates.

Preface

"As you think, so you are!"

King Solomon

Have you ever wondered what you are thinking when you are doing what you are doing? Have you ever taken the time to consider how your mindset is formed? Have you ever stopped to consider how your mindset impacts your day-to-day work? Have you ever done a deep dive into how your past informs your present? To answer these questions and many more, let me introduce you to three (of many) clients who have used the material in this book to do deep, reflective work around their mindset to bridge the gap between what they are doing and what they would like to do vs. what they are thinking and what they would like to think.

-Bill-

When Bill came to my office, it was not the first time we had talked. We met numerous times via numerous venues. We tried the virtual meetings, but face-to-face was more enriching for us both. This meeting was one of our bi-weekly sessions, but yielded some fruit he didn't see coming. It is, however, a result of what often happens over and over when gap analysis is done intentionally. Bill's example also does an excellent job of illustrating for us the focus of this book and demonstrates what King Solomon was stating centuries ago. Bill had entered the office and started his conversation, as we see below. We will soon discover that, as Bill thinks, so is Bill.

"I think I may be in trouble with my superintendent." (Bill was a principal who worked for a school district client.) The opening statement did not surprise me. I had heard him say something similar many times before as we worked together. He seemed to have this consciousness of times where he perceived that he did not perform at his best, or, better, at the benchmark of others. After he explained the impetus for this specific declaration, I asked him if he noticed that this was a typical occurrence in our work. (His starting numerous sessions with a negative rumination of some possible failed event was more than a pattern. It seemed to be a window into his heart.)

Bill paused and acknowledged this was a common occurrence. He then asked, "Why do I do that? Where does this come from? Is it from my parents?" Those were all good questions. After thirty-plus years of executive leadership coaching, you would have thought I would have had an answer for all three of Bill's inquiries. Yet, I just stared (I often find that silence with a client can convey more wisdom than if I open my mouth and make something up).

Our conversation for the rest of that session was set. We centered on the possibilities of *why* Bill starts conversations that way. We eventually drew a conclusion to the thought that Bill believes he does not measure up when he is supposed to measure up. At the end of the session, we were no closer to finding out the 'why' of the pattern; however, as Bill left, I asked him to consider any story from his past that might be contributing to this mindset. He promised he would. I walked him to the door and watched him drive away. I wondered what story was at the core of his mindset. What story would cause him to think the way he thought about his work product?

I was expecting to wait until we meet again in a few weeks to dig back into his mindset stories. However, I didn't have to wait that long. My phone rang 15 minutes later. It was Bill. He was driving. I detected a slight edge of emotion in his voice. He pulled over and unveiled to me a simple historical memory that would give him a significant key to unlocking his mindset mystery. It would be the reason behind his almost constant obsession that he was always failing others. Bill didn't realize that what he was *currently doing* was being impacted by what he was *constantly thinking*.

-Julie-

Julie had a desire to see things done right. But she also had to take care of those around her. She would far too often step in and take care of people by doing their work in the *right* way. She was, and is, by all accounts, a *high performer*. We had one intake session and one group session (a leadership cohort), and she came forward immediately, wanting to change this tendency in her leadership to always help those she leads. When I was teaching the material in this book to her cohort, she didn't hesitate when I asked for a volunteer to walk through this material. She stated she wanted to stop always taking care of others and jumping in and doing their work. She didn't know why she always stepped in to take care of others, but she knew she wanted to stop doing it. After a few conversations, Julie realized it was not out of necessity that she was caring for others. She soon realized it was about the work they were doing. She simply didn't want the work to fail. She was much more willing to give of herself and sacrifice her own time and energy rather than let the goals and outcomes of the organization flounder.

In our second one-on-one coaching session conversation, Julie had been working on the change matrix (introduced in Parts 2 & 3). She was taught the enclosed material in the group work a few weeks prior with her cohort. When she came online for our following virtual one-on-one coaching session, she was more than excited.

"I could not wait to talk to you today. I am going through this stuff, and I think I really found out what it is that is impacting me to want to care for everyone and everything thing." Although Julie was trying to hide it, I could hear the energy in her voice and see the emotion in her eyes. It would not take long to see why she was so elated. As she went through the various change matrix phases (to be explained), she was eager to unpack her findings. It wasn't until she visited a series of stories of her early life that she was able to find the meaning of her current behavior. It was (is) an amazing story of reflection and/or introspection. As she unfolded the story, what I learned more about her explained the puzzle she gave me during her intake session. I immediately saw the connection to her current mindset pattern. The most important thing was that she also saw it. Prior to this moment, she didn't realize that what she was currently doing was being highly impacted by what she was thinking.

-Ken-

By all accounts, Ken was a very good leader. His experiences over the years in the HR world had given him many opportunities to reflect and learn about his own leadership style and structure. He had hired many (too many) in an industry that, by nature, has too much turnover. This was true on a larger scale currently due to the result of the Covid-19 crisis. From my viewpoint, his capacity was quite high, and his coachability was in overdrive. He wanted to learn. He wanted to grow. When I first met him, I thought he could and should be doing my job. His years in the HR world had him well prepared to recognize the need for not only a *skill set* match but also a *mindset* match.

However, when we met to talk about his reflections on his *own* mindset, he had come to what he thought was a dead end. Instead, after just a short time, it turned out to be an epiphany that would not only solve a problem, but it would also give him the idea for a new tool. This new tool would be an innovative idea that he could use to enhance his HR world and promote his organization. He didn't realize that what he was *thinking* was restricting him from *doing* something that had been a passion in his heart for many years. He wanted to be creative. But because of what he had been taught and learned to think about, the creative spirit was hindering him from being the creative person he wanted to become. What was the result of this deep dive into his mindset? Within minutes of unlocking the door to his past, he was about to become an innovative and creative leader for the future.

As we dive into the work of genuine gap analysis, be aware that there are no stories of your past that are exempt and/or insignificant from contributing to the mindset of your present. This book is about using a system of discovery to find out how the archetypal imprints (to be further explained) of our past contribute to the performance of our present and future. The design of this book is to first help the reader discover their own past stories (archetypal imprints) for the purpose of recognizing and bridging their own mindset gaps. Yet, the material is also intended to help any leader who has hired someone who is now presenting a mindset gap, and it also teaches how to create an Individual Development Plan (IDP) to bridge them toward better understanding and better organization fit. Additionally, this material can assist any organization regarding their hiring and onboarding processes, to begin with, gap analysis, rather than after when we might find we have bigger gaps than we first realized (this is Dr. Tubbergen's focus in Part 4).

After a brief introduction, we will cover three key barriers that can often hinder the discovery of our gaps. Then, the book is divided into four parts:

Part 1 – Understanding how a mindset is formed – *The ever-changing and moving historical river of past experiences and accumulated knowledge.* In this section, we will simply use a simple model to understand some basic thoughts about how a mindset is formed and what makes it difficult to add transformational work to the transactional work we do with others.

Part 2 – Understanding how our archetypal stories impact our mindsets – In this section, we will dive into the understanding of archetypes and specifically show twelve archetypal imprints (six archetypal pairs) that contribute to our mindset. We will unfold specific beliefs, values, passions, purposes, and fears; they each contribute to our thinking and, thus, our behaviors and/or decisions.

Part 3 – Undoing the matrix of our mindsets (a step-by-step, systematic method to change your and/or staff's mindsets) – In this section, we will introduce and illustrate a process that allows us to dig deeper into our own mindsets and how to use the past stories of our lives to transform our thinking rather than to simply be sub-consciously control our thinking (and subsequent behaviors).

Part 4 – Untraditional application to organizational staffing and best-fit strategies – In this section, Dr. Lori Tubbergen Clark will give us very practical stories and applications to bring Parts 1, 2, and 3 alive regarding the hiring process. Be prepared to change your mindset as Lori unfolds for you both the horrors of a bad fit and the glories of a great fit.

Introduction

A cognitive corral preventing mindset change.

"Ponder the path of your feet; then all your ways will be sure."

–King Solomon

Have you ever wanted to change the way you think but can't seem to do it? Have you ever been told to change the way you think and found it an impossible or challenging task? Or have you been asked why you think the way you think, and you don't know why?

The English word *ponder*, in the Hebrew language, means *to make level*. Interestingly, when it is used in the Hebrew language, it is often used in the context of *leveling a road*. We might wonder if we would translate their word for *leveling a road* into our English word, *ponder*? However, we have a slang way of saying the same thing. Have you ever stated to someone or heard someone say, "You need to be more *levelheaded!*" What we are saying in that phrase is to get your mindset correct…to level out the thoughts in your mind, and think straight…like a smooth road. If we want to walk on a great path for our feet, we need to do some real, genuine, *levelheaded* pondering. We need to level out our mindsets that are often beset by possible bumps, sorted debris, and/or potholes created by the storms and explosions of life's walk.

To level out the mindset road, we need to ponder some areas of our mindset that might prevent the work. Rather than being free to ponder, we are often hindered and fenced in by those very boulders and/or holes we are attempting to identify and possibly change. There are many barriers to deep mindset work, but I would like to present to you the following for you to ponder. We need to identify any areas that might first prevent us from deeper pondering the mindset work we will be called upon to do later in this book.

A Cognitive Corral Preventing Our Mindset Change

PAST COGNITIVE ANCHORS

(The subconscious patterns that *imprint a benchmark* we think we should obtain!)

PRESENT ASSUMED CONSTRAINTS

(The subconscious assumptions *that constrain us* from doing what we think we should do!)

OUR COLLECTIVE AND PERSONAL *OCHYROMA*

(The subconscious *traits and/or skill sets* we rely on to empower us to reach our desired anchor!)

If we are going to be serious about reflecting and possibly changing our own mindset, the mindset of those who we lead, or even identifying the mindset of those we might hire, we will have to wrap our minds around the above cognitive framing.

When we attempt to do reflective work, the path is not always pleasant. It seems the deeper we dive into changing the mindset, the more past hurt and/or complications we find. Most people don't want to go deep because it is hard work. But if we want to go higher in the future, we may have to go deeper into the past. When doing that deep dive, however, we are often confronting our cognitive anchors, our assumed constraints, and our personal ochyroma (defined and explained shortly). Let's start with a basic understanding and some examples to give us clarity. As you go through the next pages, you might want to take out a journal and record what is coming in and out of your mindset. (That is the point of this work.)

Cognitive Anchors

As stated in the above graphic, I am using the following definition when using the term *cognitive anchor* in this book: *The* subconscious patterns that *imprint a benchmark* we think we should obtain! Let me give you a personal cognitive anchor that my mom imprinted on my subconscious when I was younger.

When I was in 6th or 7th grade, my mom came into my bedroom and told me to pack my bags because she was divorcing my dad. My dad was a preacher who pounded the pulpit on Sundays but turned that on my older brothers on the weekdays. I think my mom was trying to rescue me from that same pathway. I really didn't even know what the word divorce meant. In my young life (early 60s), I didn't know anyone who was divorced, much less a wife divorcing her *pastor* husband. What she should have said was, "David, I am divorcing your dad so that you will be safe." That would have been great. However, what she said that day (and multiple days later to tell the entire world why she divorced Paul) was, "David, I am divorcing your dad so that you will be a **preacher or teacher.** My mom was a middle school English teacher for thirty-plus years. Apparently, in her mindset, the only choices I should have for an occupation was *preacher* or *teacher*. As I stated, I heard that statement repeatedly. To say that it was part of my mindset for numerous years would be a great understatement. At the time of this publication, I am 69 years old. That means I have had this cognitive anchor in my mindset for decades. Becoming a preacher or teacher was (and still is, to some extent) a cognitive anchor, an imprint benchmark that I thought I had to achieve to become who I was meant to be. If I failed to do either of those two occupations, I would not only disappoint my mother (who does that?), but it would also mean she divorced Paul for no good reason. There is no way my mom intentionally did this to create a cognitive corral for me. Yet, one side of my cognitive corral is this cognitive anchor.

We all have these anchors in our mindsets. Anchors are very powerful regarding the way we think. In fact, retailers love to create anchoring mindsets for us regarding our purchasing habits. My wife often falls into this anchoring entanglement. When she walks into her favorite department store, and sees a little black dress in her size on a mannequin and sees the price the store set as $100.00. But she does not buy the dress at that moment. This retailer will have that same dress off the mannequin in a couple of weeks and on the sale rack. It will then be marked down by 50%. However, my wife will not pay $50.00 either. She is a smart woman. After her last shopping episode at this retailer, she was given a $15.00 coupon, the same as cash, on her next purchase. She will walk out of that store only paying $35.00 for that same dress she saw a few weeks earlier tagged for $100. When later that evening, she models it for me, she will invariably ask, "What do you think of my $100 dress that I bought for $35.00?" That is her mindset. I am a smart man, however, and don't say what I am thinking. Rather, I say, "Sweetheart, you look hot. Since you did such a good job of saving money, I am going to take you out to dinner tonight. And we can go to a fancy place with that money you saved. In fact, we will go inside this time and avoid the drive-through." That is not what I am thinking in my head, however. I am thinking, "That is probably a $3.00 dress you paid $32.00 too much for that was made in some sweatshop in some foreign country." I would never say that aloud to her, however. When she finally sells that dress in a yard sale for $0.35, she will turn to me and say, "That was a $100 dress!" Why? Because this retailer has mastered the art of anchoring and setting fictional benchmarks, they want us to believe are true values. They are not. Nor was the anchor my mom gave him when I was young. It was not true. But I believed it for years, anyhow.

This anchoring is true in each of our own minds. We often express our decisions about the things of life based upon our anchoring. Look at some of these quotes found in a random search on the internet:

"I think there is a world market for maybe five computers."

–Thomas Watson Sr., president of IBM, 1943.

Cognitive Anchor: **Computers serve a fixed purpose and are a certain size**!

"There is no reason for any individual to have a computer in his home."

–Ken Olsen, Digital Equipment Corp., 1977

Cognitive Anchor: **Computers are for a certain purpose**!

Or just consider what was said about the iPhone when it first came out:

"The iPhone is nothing more than a luxury bauble that will appeal to a few gadget freaks."

–Matthew Lynn, *Bloomberg*

Cognitive Anchor: **Everyday people don't like gadgets**!

"There is a low demand for converged all-in-one devices. Only 31% of Americans surveyed said they wanted a device with multiple capabilities."

-The Guardian-

Cognitive Anchor: **Americans know what they want and are always right**!

"No stylus is provided."

–Edward Baig, *USA Today*

Cognitive Anchor: **A person's finger is not feasible for small computer screens**!

"Is there a toaster that also knows how to brew coffee? There is no such combined device, because it would not make anything better than an individual toaster or coffee machine. It works the same way with the iPod, the digital camera or mobile phone: it is important to have specialized devices."

—Jon Rubinstein, former iPod creator.

Cognitive Anchor: **One device isn't designed to accomplish more than one thing**!

(By the way, it should be noted that when Steve Jobs broke this *cognitive anchor,* he almost caused the entire death of the Apple iPod division.)

Obviously, if we knew then what we know now, we would all sound and look smarter. Imagine this *cognitive anchor* stated by the Allied Armies commander in World War One, Ferdinand Foch:

"Airplanes are interesting toys but of no military value."

Cognitive Anchor: **Airplanes are only for crop dusting**!

Imagine the cognitive anchor you might develop during a leadership change. You were used to the past leader's leadership style. The new leader has a different style. Now it is tough to follow this new style because you have many *cognitive anchors* on what it means to follow and what it means to do work under the past leader. Imagine if you followed a leader that was highly hierarchical and structured. If that leader is replaced by a leadership style based upon a *distributive-leadership* model and a *leveling* of all structures, you might have some struggles as you follow the new leader.

In the aftermath of Covid-19, we have heard repeatedly we want things to go back to *normal*. The *normal* people are seeking is an established *cognitive anchor* they are used to. That gives them comfort. One of the *cognitive anchors* that was moved during the worldwide pandemic was the working from home vs. working at the office...the on-site brick-and-mortar building vs. a virtual office. This is a current debate that is still smoldering in our organizational culture fires. How you view this *cognitive anchor* might elevate your position in the marketplace with some organizations, but it might crush it in others. Allowing someone to work from home might elevate an organization and allow it to attract the best talent, but it might leave someone on an island. This is a key *cognitive anchor* that is impacting how we change or challenge our mindsets about work and the work experience.

Anchoring is a real fence that forms one side of our *cognitive corral*. Anchoring can push us into false assumptions and untenable arguments. As we attempt to engage in mindset work, it might be wise for you to consider your own *cognitive anchors*. What benchmarks are you holding that you believe cannot be moved or changed about yourself? Or do you have a staff member you lead that you believe will NEVER change because they are _____? Are you hindering your movement because a *cognitive anchor* is holding back how you are dreaming and your creativity (see Ken's story from the *Preface*)? What have you *learned* in life that you might want to consider unlearning?

If you are in education, working with children, you are referred to as working in the field of pedagogy. Most teachers spend most of their lives teaching children something that the child does not know. As a leadership coach, I am more in the field of andragogy. I spend most of my time teaching adults to let go of something they learned from the past that is hindering their mindset shift for the present and/or future. Some *cognitive anchors* are beliefs we must consider *unlearning*. Not all *cognitive anchors* are unhealthy. But we need to reflect on just how they impact our mindset. I, personally, had to *unlearn* the anchor that I could only be a preacher or teacher in life. As we further unpack the story of Bill, Julie, and Ken from the Preface, you will discover they, too, had to *unlearn* something from their past to change their mindset for the future.

We should be warned, however, that we don't always have to throw out an entire *cognitive anchor*. We may only have to *unlearn* parts of the *anchor* and hold tight to the parts that remain. I could be a preacher or teacher, but I needed to let go of the fact that I had attached a statement from my mom (made in frustration) that those two occupations were the ONLY choices I had in life. We need to be careful not to toss out the baby with the bathwater. Our desire should be to identify our *cognitive anchors* and what parts need to be tossed, what parts need to be held onto, and/or what parts may have to be re-written.

Before you move to the next section, consider doing the following work regarding your own *cognitive anchor(s)*:

Working through a cognitive anchor					
Identify a cognitive anchor in your life:	**Where did you learn it?**	**What part of it might still be true for you today?**	**What part must you re-write?**	**What part must be unlearned?**	**What part should you throw away?**

Assumed Constraints

I am using the following definition when using the term *assumed constraints* in this book: The subconscious assumptions ***that constrain us*** from doing what we think we should do! Whereas a *cognitive anchor* often begins with an *it should* type of phrase (meaning, *it should look like this*), an *assumed constraint* often begins with a, *we can't, because* (meaning, *we can't do that because…*) type of phrase. *Cognitive anchors* are what we think it should look like. *Assumed constraints* are often the reasons we can't move either toward an *anchor* or away from an *anchor*. Let's return to *my-mother-said-to-me* story.

After my mom divorced my dad and left the house with all the belongings we could fit in her car, we moved into a trailer park. It was not a *modular home community*. It was a trailer park with a trailer with wheels. We didn't have much, to say the least. On top of this economic issue, I immediately began to suffer in school, and my grades were a visual sign of that struggle. I often listened to my mom tell others (over and over) that the reason she divorced Paul was so that I would be a preacher of teacher. But my mind would focus on the fact that we had little money and I had very poor grades. At one point, in a time of sudden candor, I shouted at my mom and said, "Have you seen my grades? Do you see where we live? How can I ever be a preacher or teacher?" You see, she had a *cognitive anchor* that I should be a preacher or teacher. Truthfully though, we had no way to pay for it, and I was a terrible student. Those two thoughts were my *assumed constraints*. She wanted me to do this (*cognitive anchor*), but I didn't think I could because of that (*assumed constraint*).

> (**NOTE:** *Do you see the other cognitive anchors in my logic, however? I had two. One was that it is my mother's job to pay my way to college. That was how I thought it should be. I would later, however, join the U.S. Army. After serving my years, I would later be able to attend college on the G.I. Bill. The second cognitive anchor was that I thought only the best students with good grades could go to college, and I was not a good student. In fact, my anchor was that I thought I was dumb. Again, God changed that through His grace, using the hammer of the U.S. Army. They hammered the dumb anchor out and replaced it with a thought that "...you can do it." When I left the military, my mom was still standing there, still asking, "Preacher or teacher?" But, at that point, no assumed constraint to hold me back. Letting go of those assumed constraints changed my path.*)

Think of a horse brought to a hitching post to be secured. The horse has the power to pull away from the post. Yet, it has learned from the very beginning that the line tied to the post is attached to the bit in the horse's mouth. When the horse was young, it would attempt to pull away. The bit, the bridle and the rein are all introduced to the horse at an early age. Those pieces of equipment taught the horse they were constrained. Therefore, they don't attempt to pull away. In fact, even if the horse is not securely tied to the hitching post, they will seldom attempt to leave on their own. They simply, as before, *assumed* they are *constrained*.

The idea of *self-constraints* has been around for quite some time. We hinder ourselves from growth because we only see limits in our life and not the possibilities. We *assume* we are tied to a hitching post. There is a long list of these *constraints*, but here are some I recently unearthed while working with a transportation department of a local k-12 school district:

1. We don't have enough money.

2. We don't have enough time.

3. We don't have enough talent.

4. My leaders won't let me do that (said the team).

5. The staff will resist that (said by the leader).

6. We are too busy.

7. I don't have a degree.

8. I don't have any authority to do that.

9. I can't do that because I am _____.

10. I tried that once and failed and will fail again.

Obviously, we must admit some of these might be a real constraint. When we are doing *gap analysis*, we must recognize that sometimes there is a real gap, and no bridge, no matter how well constructed, can close the gap. There are times when we do not have enough money, time, talent, etc. There are real constraints on people because of who they are, what their background is, and even their ethnicity based upon society's bias. Those are not *assumed*; they are *real*. The challenge we have is our ability to discern the *real* from the *assumed*. (They both should always be addressed.). This is why the *assumed constraint* is one part of our *cognitive corral* that is holding us back and preventing the bridge from being built to close gaps.

Anyone who has done anything great in our society regarding leadership has decided to not allow *assumed constraints* to stop them. Let me give you a few to consider:

"So, we went to Atari and said, 'Hey, we've got this amazing thing, even built with some of your parts, and what do you think about funding us? Or we'll give it to you. We just want to do it. Pay our salary, we'll come work for you.' And they said 'No.' "

This was related by Stephen Jobs, Apple Computer co-founder, on his attempts in the mid-1970s to get Atari interested in his and Steve Wozniak's personal computer.

Assumed Constraint: **Atari thought, "Your ideas won't work here because you have no credentials."**

In 1965, Yale University undergraduate Frederick W. Smith wrote a term paper that invented an industry and changed what's possible. He proposed a system specifically designed to accommodate time-sensitive shipments such as medicine, computer parts, and electronics. Smith's professor apparently didn't see the revolutionary implications of his thesis, and the paper received just an average grade.

That was the day FedEx was born!

Assumed Constraint: **Time and space don't allow us to deliver packages all over the world fast.**

"Aside from Web speed issues, the iPhone has two serious flaws. First, it's awkward to handle. At 4 1/2 by 2 3/8 inches, it's half an inch wider than my regular cell phone—too wide to hold comfortably. And the iPhone is slippery—too easy to drop."

–Mike Himowitz, The Baltimore Sun

Assumed Constraint: **People have small hands. People can't adapt to new things.**

There are times when, yes, a *constraint* is real, and there are times when it is only *assumed* to be a constraint. The *cognitive corral* is fortified when we simply do not distinguish between the two. Here are a few questions to ask yourself about a constraint to determine if it is a *real* or an *assumed constraint*.

Question #1 – Where did I learn this *constraint*? Identifying the source where this mindset came from. Identification of the *constraint* is an important step in understanding it and distinguishing between the *real* and the *assumed*. We can often know the credibility of something when we know the original source code of the thought. Not everything we learn comes from bad sources. But not everything we have learned comes from good sources, either. Learning and adopting a *constraint* is what builds it into our mindset. Unlearning it and rejecting it can be tough if the source for it comes from a trusted entity (i.e., a mother?). But, failing to ask the question of where it came from is not being disloyal to even the most trusted source. Asking the question allows us to analyze and improve our mindset. Not asking the question is being disloyal to your own reflection.

Question #2 – Is the constraint I am believing based upon groupthink? There are probably many versions of Christopher Columbus discovering the Americas. But it is doubtful he would have set sail had he listened to the crowd. The same would be true of President Kennedy wanting to send someone to the moon, Henry Ford wanting to create the combustible engine, Alexander Graham Bell wanting to talk over the phone, Elon Musk wanting to create an electric car, and/or any other great invention we have today. The crowd can often be right. But if we listen to the crowd, we might be held in check by an *assumed constraint mantra* that has crushed many great ideas with the tragic line: *No one has ever done this before*!

Question #3 – Is the constraint based upon my own self-comfort? This might be one of the hardest questions to ask when regarding *assumed constraints*. We may not have learned it, and we may not have the crowd telling us we cannot do it. But we do have an inner voice that tells us to stay in a comfortable lane of life. The *this is how I have always done it* might be the lamest excuse for holding us back in life. If we want to grow and learn and close gaps, we will have to stop being comfortable with our existence and be willing to step into other lanes of life. We cannot expect to build a bridge over a gap if we do not want to move away from our comfortable side of the gap.

Question #4 – Is the constraint because I am avoiding doing hard work? It takes work to build a bridge. It is not typically our fear of deciding to change that holds us back. It is our failure to want to do the work once the decision is made. We often delay the decision or complain about the decision so that we don't have to do the work the change requires. We would much rather criticize the decision than be critical of our work ethic surrounding the decision. We often use an *assumed constraint* as an excuse to avoid the challenging work we know should be done. We like to say we are constrained even when we are not because it allows us to sit back, relax and save energy. Hard work is often the avenue of change and closing a gap. However, it is seldom paved, and it is often walked alone with sweat on our brow.

Question #5 – Is the constraint a fear of wanting to look deeper into yourself? I am going to write more about fear later in this book but suffice it to say here that when we don't want to go deeper, we might not be able to overcome an *assumed constraint*. You can't really do questions #1-4 if you fear looking into your mindset. This book is all about self-reflection. We cannot unlearn an *assumed constraint* without knowing what we are thinking deeper into ourselves. So many people simply go through life living on the surface and avoiding the tough introspection required for a more vibrant and growing life. Leaders can't be like other people. The best leaders are primarily reflective people. In fact, after 30 years of coaching leaders, I would say that is one of the most important distinguishing characteristics of great leaders. Poor and average leaders point to others as the reason something is not working. Great leaders look inside and do the deeper, reflective work needed to make a change that will impact the problem, the solution and/or the entire team, in a positive manner.

If we want to overcome our *assumed constraints,* we must ask some tough questions. The answers we find in those questions will become the girders for the bridge over any identified mindset gaps. Before we move away from the thought of our *assumed constraints*, use the following simple approach to work through your own *assumed constraints*:

Working through an assumed constraint					
Identify an assumed constraint in your life:	Where did you learn it?	What part of it might still be true for you today?	What part must you re-write?	What part must be unlearned?	What part should you throw away?

Your Personal Ochyroma

I love to study words from other languages. I think word choice in our conversations is highly underrated regarding our leadership work (see my third book: TRUST! Using Archetypal Language to Repair Broken Trust). When I come across a word from a language I have never learned, I like to dig into the word to see how it is used, was used and/or could be used. With that thought in mind, let me introduce you to the Greek word: *Ochyroma* (phonetically pronounced, Oh-Hear-Roma). The Greeks do an excellent job with language. They have a much richer language than our English. For instance, we have one word in English for the word love. They have many. We might say we love our friends, we love our family, and we love our spouse. But they might say they *philia* (affectionate love) their friend. Or they *storge* (unconditional, familial love) their family. Or they *agape* (self-sacrificing love) their spouse … or, even they *eros* (romantic, passionate, erotic love) their spouse.

That is what draws me to the word *ochyroma*. This word was used in two ways in the Ancient Greek world. Like our English words, the context of the sentence determines the use of this Greek word. The word basically means a *stronghold*. Here is one author's definition of the word:

> ὀχύρωμα **ochyrōma;** *from a remote derivative of echo (meaning to fortify, through the idea of holding safely); a castle (figuratively, argument): — stronghold.*

> (W.E. Vine – Expository Dictionary)

The word used in most context would be a *stronghold* you run to for safety. You and I might think of a safe house in our home. In the ancient world, an *ochyroma* could be a large castle or a small cave. If you lived in a village during the early Greek culture and a pillaging army came to raid your community, you would run to the village *ochyroma* for safety. The *ochyroma* would be stocked with plenty of wine, cheese, water, and fruit to sustain you during this invasion. You would wait until the army pillaged your town and then left with your ducks and chickens. Once the army left, you would come out of the *ochyroma* and rebuild your town. So, an *ochyroma* is a stronghold we run to for safety.

Let me illustrate my personal *ochyroma*. Before my mother divorced my father, but after my older brothers had left the house, my dad came to my room one evening and said:

Dad: "David, get up. You must go down to the pump-house with me. The pump is out, and I have to fix it. You need to hold the flashlight."

Note: This will date me, but we pumped water out of the nearby creek to wash our clothes. Yes, I am old.

David: "Okay, dad. (Not very enthusiastic.)

We walked the one-hundred yards, or so, down the hill to the pump house. It was late summer. It was hot, and the mosquito population was thriving. The closer we were to the pump-house, the more these little bugs began to torment us.

Dad: "Now hold the flashlight," he commanded me as he knelt to start the work. He was wearing a white, muscle man-type t-shirt which he used to show off his physique but also made the perfect backdrop for these little bugs. The mosquitoes began to land on his back like it was Atlanta International Airport.

In my defense for what happens next, I have to say I was only about 10-11. Instead of holding the flashlight steady like I was told, I began to shine the light on his back and attacked the mosquitoes with a vengeance. I think I might have been channeling the abuse I saw my brothers endure from my dad. I started hitting his back a little harder and harder, and the light became increasingly eradicated. What would happen next would be a major contributor (if not the sole contributor) to my personal *ochyroma*, however.

My dad turned around and continued to stoop at my height. He took the flashlight and shined it right into his eyes. (To this day, I don't know how he could see me.) He stared at me and said the following:

"David, you will never be more talented than anyone else. You will never be more skilled than others. You will never be smarter than others. And you certainly won't be better looking than others (which I thought was funny since it was often said that I looked like my dad). But you can work harder than anyone else. Now hold the damn flashlight!"

At that moment, my dad said a lot of rough things to me in a terribly angry and rough tone (his normal tone). You might think I walked away from that experience broken, hurt, and scarred for life. But not really. Did you catch what my dad told me that day? My dad had never told me anything before or after that regarding my potential. But, on that hot, mosquito-infested summer night, my dad told me that I could *outwork anyone*. He taught me what would become my personal *ochyroma*. I learned that day I could outwork anyone. How did I know that? Because my DAD TOLD ME I COULD. That *outwork anyone mindset* would become the stronghold of my life that I would run to no matter the situation. If a pillaging army comes into my path, my lane, my journey, I just outwork it. That is my *ochyroma*.

The second meaning of *ochyroma*, however, could change everything in this scenario. The word, depending on context, could also mean *prison*. If someone did something bad, you might see them put into an *ochyroma*. They would be locked up in a stronghold, but not one to their own liking. And not one full of water, wine, cheese, and fruit for their creature comforts.

Let us go back to this word picture of a pillaging army coming into your village. When the invasion started, you would run to your cave, castle, or chamber (your *ochyroma*) and seek safety. You have plenty of water, cheese, wine, and fruit to outlast these invaders. Or so you thought. When you look out the slot of your *ochyroma*, however, you see that this army also brought their own water, cheese, wine, and fruit. Also, they brought much more than you have stored. You suddenly discover that they did not come to pillage your village. They came to besiege your village. Your *ochyroma* is no longer a stronghold. It has become your prison. Where you ran for safety has now become your suffering.

When I was 55 years old, I had a heart attack. Why? There were some minor physiological reasons, but also because of this stronghold in my life. In all the years before that event, I would attempt to outwork everyone. That *ochyroma* became my prison. The trait I thought would always be there as my safety had indeed become my suffering. It took that moment in my life, with some introspection, to identify that what was my stronghold could also become my prison.

A little girl sees her mother in the kitchen and asks her mother what she is doing. The mother says, "I am baking cupcakes for our neighbor lady. She is sick." The little girl asks if she could help. Mother not only let her help, but she also let her take the cupcakes to the neighbor lady. At the front door of the house, the neighbor pats the little girl's head and states, "You are such a great little girl for making me these cupcakes." At that moment, an *ochyroma* is born in the little girl's life. She knows she has worth if she makes baked goods to give to those in need.

Later in life, this little girl would grow to become a woman with one mission. She would spend hours in the kitchen baking in order to give the baked goods away. She decides to turn this endeavor into a business. However, before long, she is spending every weekday and every weekend baking. What was a stronghold to give her meaning and purpose would, eventually, become her prison.

My stories from my youth that revolve around my mom helped me, unwillingly, to develop some of my *cognitive anchors* and *assumed constraints*. The pumphouse story with my dad gave me further input into my life. The pump-house event produced a powerful *ochyroma* that did (and still does) become a prison that not only prevented my growth and hindered my zest for life, but came close to killing me...literally. That is not true for all strongholds. However, an *ochyroma* in our lives can severely hinder our mindset growth.

Whereas a *cognitive anchor* is what we think something should be, and an *assumed constraint* is something we think holds us back from achieving our (or other's) cognitive anchor, our *ochyroma* is the trait or skill set we often employ to overcome our constraint to achieve our anchors.

We all have an *ochyroma* (often more than one) that we run to for safety. Gap analysis is about identifying your *ochyroma(s)*. It is about learning how to unpack it and claim its stronghold, and to avoid the prison. The *ochyroma* is not a terrible thing in our lives. For many, it is a stronghold for a good reason and for much good. However, when we fail to recognize the prison side of an *ochyroma*, it captures us. It prevents us from growth. It hinders the bridging of the gaps we find in our lives and the lives of others. It creates around us a cognitive corral that stops growth.

As we move forward in our gap analysis work, this cognitive corral will be exposed for what it is, a series of fence lines that prevent growth, hinders our forward movement and robs us of our vigor. The following pages will give us tools to deal with each of these components. However, moving forward with the work on the next pages can easily be derailed when we fail to look at this corral. If you are willing to bust out of your compound and find a wide-open territory to explore, turn the next page and start knocking down *cognitive anchors, assumed constraints* and your personal *ochyroma*.

Here are three questions to ask yourself regarding the identification of your personal *ochyroma*:

Question #1 – When push comes to shove, what is your first response? Where do you turn to? Some possible considerations (there could be more than one):

- o Being positive – Always believing

- o Seeing and identifying dangers

- o Rolling up your sleeves to help others

- o Rolling up your sleeves to conquer the problem

- o Using your imagination and innovative ideas

- o Gathering your team and making sure everyone is pulling together

- o Dismantling whatever is not working to make way for something new to be done

- o Taking the ideas of others and making them into tangible tools

- o Structuring everything and everyone

- o Transforming everyone's thinking

- o Using your knowledge and expertise

- o Making sure you and everyone are not taking things to seriously

Question #2 – Which of these types of stories give you energy and appeal to you? Some considerations (there could be more than one):

- o Stories that offer hope despite the obvious dangers

- o Stories of caring for others by conquering challenges

- o Stories of thinking of the new while honoring the traditions of the past

- o Stores of moving away from the old and creating the new

- o Stories of changing hearts and minds to maintain a safe and structured world

- o Stores of enjoyment while learning new things

Question #3 – What is a significant memory from your childhood that still stays with you today:

We use our best trait/skill (*ochyroma*) to get over barriers (*assumed constraints*) to reach our anchored objective (*cognitive anchors*).

PAST COGNITIVE ANCHORS

(The subconscious patterns that *imprint a benchmark* we think we should obtain!)

PRESENT ASSUMED CONSTRAINTS

(The subconscious assumptions *that constrain us* from doing what we think we should do!)

OUR COLLECTIVE AND PERSONAL *OCHYROMA*

(The subconscious *traits and/or skill sets* we rely on to empower us to reach our desired anchor!)

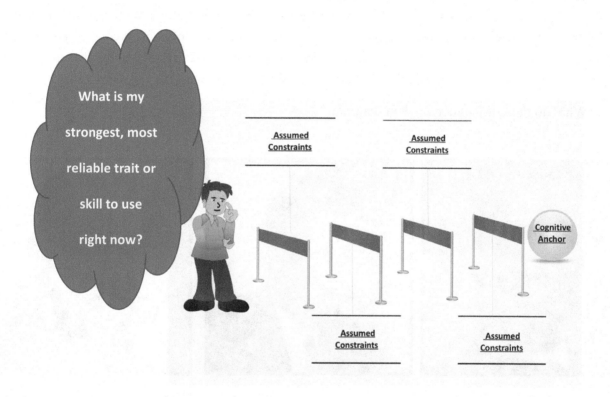

PART 1
Understanding How a Mindset is Formed

"If you realized how powerful your thoughts are, you would never think a negative thought."
–*Peace Pilgrim* Excerpt from *Switch on Your Brain,* Caroline Leaf

We often talk about the mindset as though it is right in front of us. We talk about it like it is part of our body, like the heart, the hand, or the head. But we know it is not. The mindset is not only non-tangible; it is also complicated and impossible to map out. Make a simple internet search on images of *mind mapping,* and you will walk away more confused than when you started. Since we only observe the behavior a mindset produces, it is easy to draw incomplete, unverifiable, and misdiagnosed thoughts about someone's mind. We can even draw such a wrong conclusion that we do unhealthy things.

What do these three men have in common?

You might say they are politicians. You might say they were leaders. You might say they attempted to change the minds of an entire country. All those answers would be correct answers. However, they also were all three assassinated. They attempted to change how people think. They attempted to bridge the gap by changing *cognitive anchors*, *assumed constraints*, and the *ochyroma* of others. Others did not always understand what they were thinking. Too many did not agree with what they were thinking. Their mindset went contrary to someone(s) so much that those very people decided that these leaders didn't have the right to think that way. So, they took their lives.

When we think of the highways of the mindset, we must realize that we might come across some

 people who do not understand how we think. Or we might not understand how they think. We cannot always put things in boxes, columns, rows, and logic that everyone can understand. The *anchors*, *constraints* and *strongholds* that cost these leaders their lives are unexplainable and unfathomable. And, if you don't mind this very unfair comparison between these great leaders and us, people will not often understand our (your) vision for change, either. We may not be

physically assassinated, but we might have our reputations, our decisions, our careers and/or our innovative ideas terminated by those who resist change. Nelson Mandela's mindset was so different from his culture that he spent 27 years in prison. That did not change his mindset. He went on to become the father of modern-day South Africa.

It might be wise to start with how a mindset might work. Understanding how a mindset might work would help us understand the mindset of others and, if needed, attempt to change their minds. Look at the mindset map on the next page. I would prefer you think about it before you move on to read what I am trying to say, explain or emphasize. I think it is best you see the entire diagram before I break down the components within it and explain how I believe it applies to this gap analysis work. When we have a large gap, it can simply mean a bad fit for a member of our team. It can, additionally, become serious and cost us valuable time, energy and even the health of our lives and occupations. How do you see a mindset form? How do you think you would map it out? What do you think this is saying? Use this blank space to map out your thoughts about how a mind is formed and how it can be mapped for understanding:

What on earth is David thinking with this diagram?

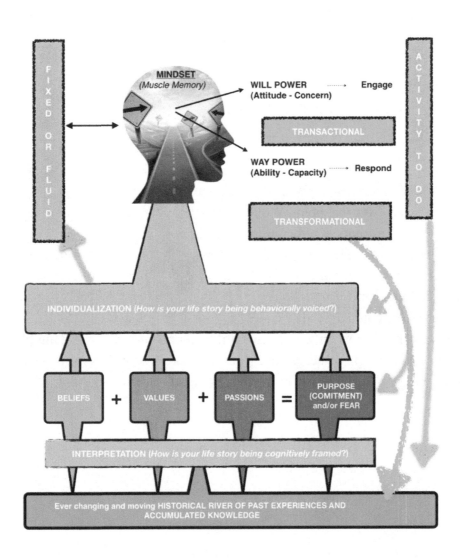

So, what are your thoughts about the above diagram? How does it compare to the one drawn out about the forming of a mindset? Record your take-a-ways in the box below. (It is important that you stop reading and do some reflective work.) What are your wonderings? Where do you see areas you think you agree with? What are areas that you see that you disagree with? What are areas that you just do not understand or are confusing? What would you change about the diagram to better reflect a mindset diagram you see in your mind?

To explain my thinking, let's start at the beginning of the diagram. Oops! Wait a minute. Where is the *starting* point? That is typically the first criticism I hear from groups I work with who are centered on this work. They always want a *starting* point. Wouldn't that be great? Wouldn't it be great to have a starting point we can use for everyone we meet to begin to understand their mindset and close the gaps? The issue with that mindset thought is that no two people are alike. Not everyone can start in the same place. The first thing you may notice about the diagram is that it appears to be circular in nature. That is somewhat how the mindset works. Some things come into our minds, and send some things go out. We then rinse and repeat daily. It would be great if we could just do a step one, step two, step three, etc. approach that fits all people the same. But that is not the case when working with the complicated and non-tangible human mind. We can't cut the mindset open in a safe place, replace a part to make it better and/or make it the way we would like and then sew it back up. We, of course, know this, but it still needs to be said.

But we must start somewhere, so let's start here:

It may be comfortable to stay on the same road each day, but it will eventually both end your trip and limit your experiences!

Many roads make many journeys!

Mindset – Muscle Memory

When we consider the mindset, we might want to consider it as a *muscle memory* system. Our minds are like patterns. We like to think in patterns. Those patterns used over time form a memory system that allows us to process and think logically (or, to others, at times, illogically). As said, the mind is non-tangible, but that does not prevent us from creating this structured thinking process. What those steeped deeply in this knowledge tell us is that the more we think about something the same way, the more that thinking acts like a muscle and forms its own structured system. It can and often does become a memory system. It becomes a muscle memory system. The take-away point for our work is that these same researchers tell us we can retrain the mind to change our memory system. We can create new forms of thinking.

Fixed or Fluid? Activities to Do (Will Power vs. Way Power)

To begin this work, we must always consider if we have a *fixed* or *fluid* mindset. It is interesting how an audience can be split if you ask whether we should have a *fixed* or *fluid* mindset. The truth is we have both. Since the answer depends on the topic, our past learning, our muscle memory and a thousand other components, we must realize the answer can be difficult to nail down. Since the entire topic of this book is about how to close the gaps in mindset work, we might think we should lean toward being more *fluid* in our mindsets. However, this is the challenge. There are many areas of our mindset where we are *fixed,* and we like it. Those areas can assure our success and create predictable outcomes. The debate rages about whether we should ever be *fixed*. The irony is that those who believe we should be constantly *fluid* in our mindset are *fixed* regarding that argument. I am not attempting to argue in favor for either one of those, in this work. I just want us to recognize that this work is often hindered by both. I am more interested in what makes the mindset *fixed* or what makes it *fluid*. That is the point of this book. If we know

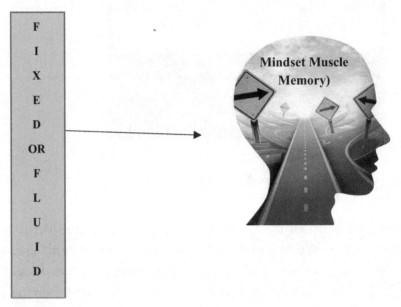

what makes a mindset *fixed* or *fluid*, we can better understand why it is that way and whether that is the cause or the hindrance of the gap we are trying to bridge.

When we talk about a *fixed* or *fluid* mindset, we often see it when we ask someone to do a particular *activity* for us. Their *fixed* or *fluid* mindset is often heightened if they think they can do the activity (they believe they have the *way* power, the *ability/capacity* to do the activity). If they think they don't have the capacity, they might switch to a *fixed* mindset quite fast. Those who lack the *ability* (an underlying perception that they CAN'T do something) do not often step up to tackle a task they are being asked to tackle.

On the other hand, they may believe they can do the activity but simply lack the *will* power to do it. They can do it but don't want to. They have some *concern* (an underlying belief they don't WANT to do something) that has changed their *attitude* toward the activity. Let me illustrate with two personal examples. These two pictures might mean something different to you than me, depending on your mindset.

If you ask me to shovel your driveway for an entire winter, I will say NO! I can shovel a driveway, but simply don't want to. I have an *attitude* challenge. On the other hand, if you asked me to slam dunk a basketball, I would be all in and would love to do it. However, I am *vertically* challenged. I am 5'8" and old. The truth is, I could never slam dunk a basketball, at any age.

The underlying story behind that comes from junior high school, during a lunch time experience. I have a *cognitive anchor* and an *assumed constraint* for both these activities. I have shoveled many driveways and don't like the activity or the snow (*cognitive anchor*). In junior high, during lunch, I tried to jump and just touch the net hanging from a basketball rim. I quickly developed an assumed constraint (well, maybe not *assumed* … but hopefully, you get my point). My thoughts toward these two activities are already fixed in the *muscle memory* of my mind. I have a *will* power problem with shoveling snow and a *way* power problem with slam dunking a basketball. This is the challenge as leaders. If we don't know the mindset of our team, we often face the same dilemma. We ask people to do more of this or less of that. Or to stop doing this, or to start doing that (these four areas are kind of a sad commentary on our role as the leader). But we don't realize that those we lead may have a muscle memory that is preventing them from wanting to tackle the task(s) we are asking them to do. We would love to engage them because of their choice. We would love them to *respond* because they can. However, if they lack either *way* power or *will* power, we can get a resistance founded and based upon the muscle memory of their mind.

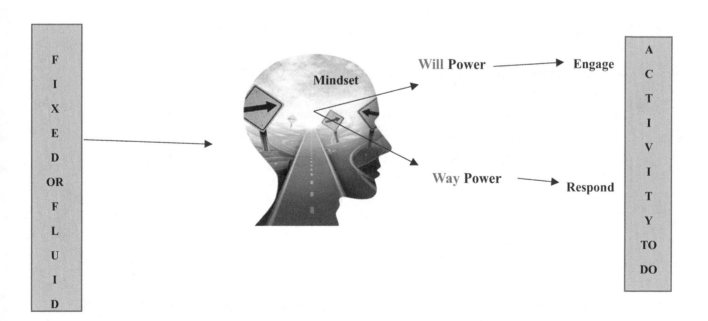

Transactional or Transformational?

As we move further into the diagram, let's talk about the area of *transactional* leadership as opposed to *transformational* leadership. My use of the terms is as follows:

Transactional Leadership	Transformational Leadership
Works with the behavior and typically wants something done.	Works with the thinking and wants something learned or thought.
Is willing to give, in order to get.	Is willing to convince, in order to get.
Wants to accomplish something with a simple transaction.	Wants to accomplish something after someone has transformed their thinking.
The conversation should lead to an outcome at some point.	The conversation is the outcome.
The change is in behavior.	The change is in thinking.
Tends to use the mindset of the past.	Tends to use the mindset of the future.

The work in this book is more on the line of *transformational* change. However, there is never an *either/or* approach to leadership regarding these two components of leadership. They should complement each other. We are constantly, as leaders, involved in both. But, under the current pace of leadership and/or life, regretfully, we tend to have less time for *transformational* work with our team. We are being forced by time pressures and outside challenges to focus solely on the *transactional* aspect of our work. Sometimes we just need things done. We want to move on and get stuff off our plate or check a box and, hopefully, get promoted and/or paid for it. We often don't even have time for the type of material in this book, or in other books like it. *Transactional* leadership is faster and, perhaps, more predictable. It is certainly more measurable. We create a transaction by agreeing to pay *this* for *that*. When *this* is done, we can see it. So, we pay *that*. It is easy. It is uncomplicated. *Transformational* work is messy. *Transformational* work is exceedingly difficult to measure. *Transformational* work does not typically have an end date. How do you know if you are done? *Transformation* is seldom DONE!

There is no objection by this author that this is a *fixed* mindset about *transactional* work. That mindset can even be a healthy mindset, at times (which, by the way, has its own *anchor*, *constraint*, and *stronghold*). However, long, systemic change is typically only accomplished by changing hearts and minds.

Both *transactional* and *transformational* are important work for leadership. It is not about which one we are doing, or which one is best. It is which one is best for the moment we are in that we can call for and assure the best results. We can do *transactional* work but never really move an organization forward. It should be less of a debate about which of the two I use and more of which of the two are needed right now. As we dive deeper into our diagram, we are going to focus more on *transformational* leadership vs *transactional*. That does not mean we will lessen the need for the *transactional*. It just means we have a *mindset* to focus on one over the other in this book.

The Ever-Flowing Thought River of Life

> Ever changing and moving HISTORICAL RIVER OF PAST EXPERIENCES AND ACCUMULATED KNOWLEDGE

Before we can really focus on transformational leadership work to identify and bridge any gaps, let's consider this unique river that runs deep in our subconscious.

Rivers are fascinating. They carry so much. Water is, of course, their main commodity. But they can also carry debris. They can carry resources. They can carry chemicals. They can carry people in canoes (and people out of canoes). Rivers supply life to the world around them. The river, however, eventually spills out into the oceans and seas, and we don't even see an impact. But there is an impact!

So, too, the *thought river* of that runs deep in our subconscious. It has many turns and twists and carries much we don't even know and/or remember. But it spills out into our lives, and when we make decisions, chart a course, and/or engage in conversation, this river pours out every drop it is carrying. Our *thought river* carries good thoughts and bad thoughts, healthy thoughts and unhealthy thoughts, all at the same time. It can carry nutrients and pollutants. It can carry dreams and deaths. All that it carries mixes and turns and unites. Like a real river, we might watch and observe; our *thought river* simply carries all things that fall into it. It typically has truly little discernment. Not without some intentionality. In fact, every activity we do simply falls into this *thought river*. It is then joined and connected to other memories. It quickly consumes a past activity and swallows it up into the currents of our minds. The words on this page and the pages before this one are all flowing and connecting in your own mind. They are beginning to intertwine with your past thoughts, activities, learning, experiences, joys, pains, laughter, and sorrow. Long after you toss this book into a box, a friend's path, or a garbage can, this activity of reading will still have some part in your thought life. Your *cognitive corral* is very much formed by the pouring out of this *thought river* into the ocean of your life.

I love the fact that our *thought river* is always changing. When I was writing my second book (*The Archetypes and the Drama of Change*), we were on a Harley trip across the country. We stopped in Yellowstone National Park. I took time to write about ten pages of that book, watching a river that ran

Activity to do

Ever changing and moving HISTORICAL RIVER OF PAST EXPERIENCES AND ACCUMULATED

alongside the highway we were traveling. The river was carrying whatever it carried past me, onto wherever it went. The river I saw at one moment was not the same configuration as what I would see only moments later. Yes, the outside of the banks was the same, but the contents of the river changed. If fact, perhaps even the banks were different because of the passing water. Whatever it contributed at that time had no immediate impact. But it would change that bank, over time. This is the same truth about what we pour into our *thought river*. In fact, we might want to further develop on what Dr. Leaf sited in her book, which was mentioned at the beginning of this section:

If we knew how all-consuming our thought river was,

We would be more discriminating in what we allowed to pour into it each day.

Whatever activity (experience or intentional learning) pours into our *thought river* eventually begins to formulate all types of shapes and patterns of thought in our mindset. One book would not be able to contain all that our *thought river* produces. We can't even write about the *most important* shapes and sizes our *thought river* might produce. Why? Because for one person, a trip to a pump house on the edge of a creek would be meaningless. To me, it created an *ochyroma* that has both propelled me forward and supplied a level of success, yet almost literally killed me. We can't underestimate the connection that is made as one story or moment or activity bumps into another story or moment or activity in our *thought river*. We must never discredit either one of them.

A key area to consider is to think about how we *interpret* these collective shapes and patterns. If we experience an event in our lives (like a worldwide pandemic) while at the same time being heavily involved with making decisions that impact the lives of others, as well as experiencing a loss in our lives, our interpretation may be different than someone who was less affected by the same events.

A question regarding *interpretation* might be asked, "How is your story being cognitively framed?" Imagine that you teach a 2–4-year-old child not to touch an electrical plug in your home. The *thought river* for this child will probably *cognitively frame* that electrical plugs are dangerous. Now let's have that same child grow up with this *cognitively framed* imprint and have her/him attend their first sleep-over with a friend, ten years later. When someone at the sleep-over attempts to plug in their iPhone 22 (we might be on that version in 10 years), this child might yell out, "*Don't touch that plug; it can kill you!*" What the child learned from their parents was a particular interpretation about electrical plugs. The other children at that sleep-over will most certainly give this child another interpretation, however. A different *cognitive framing* of electrical plugs. The childhood *interpretations* we receive are often challenged later in life. Imagine ten more years (iPhone 32), and this same child goes off to college, carrying all these *interpretations* imprinted on them by their parent(s). A professor tells the class something about this or that, and this child raises their hand to the object. The professor asks, "And where did you get that interpretation?" This child may not even know at this point. But the interpretations of their *thought river* begin to form their unique *life story*. Their life story was, is, and will continue to be *cognitively framed* by the world around them.

Recall the story about my mom and what she said that night about divorcing my dad? That was my interpretation for my *thought river*. Remember Bill from the preface and his fear of making a mistake? His interpretation of his *thought river*! Remember Julie's and Ken's stories? Their interpretation of their *thought river*. Remember that significant story I had you consider from your school days when we were considering your *ochyroma*? How do you interpret that story? How you *cognitively framed* that story would foster what we are about to consider next. The work of a leader does who is focused upon *transformation* is often challenged by these interpretations of past learning and life experiences. The real challenge might be that we are not always aware of all that is flowing in our own *thought river*, much less in the person(s) we are leading. When we do a *gap analysis,* we are seldom aware of what is in someone's *thought river* and/or their personal or learned interpretation of their life events. A key is our ability to help them and guide them through these interpretations of life. As leaders, we are often put in positions to help those we lead in their past *cognitive framing* of events. We do not always feel qualified to do this *interpretation* work. But, like it or not, it is essential when we consider the *cognitive framing* of those we lead, promote, challenge and even hire. Gap analysis work demands our ability to understand this *thought river* and what has been formed in it and by it.

INTERPRETATION (*How is your story being cognitively framed?*)

Activity to do

Ever changing and moving HISTORICAL RIVER OF PAST EXPERIENCES AND ACCUMULATED KNOWLEDGE

Beliefs > Values > Passions > Purpose (Commitments and/or Fears)

Let's go back to our diagram and select just a few of the things that come out of this *thought river* of life. The areas listed below are not suggested to be the ONLY patterns that come out of our *thought river*. They are, however, key elements we can unfold that will truly impact our *gap analysis* work.

Consider the terms in the reddish boxes below. When you first saw them in the diagram at the beginning of Part 1, what were your thoughts? Did you consider why they are in different shades of red? Did you consider the difference in definitions between *beliefs, values, passions, and purpose* (*commitment and/or fear*)? For instance, what is the difference between a *belief* and a *value*? Do you see how each of these might contribute to our mindset? In what way do they contribute?

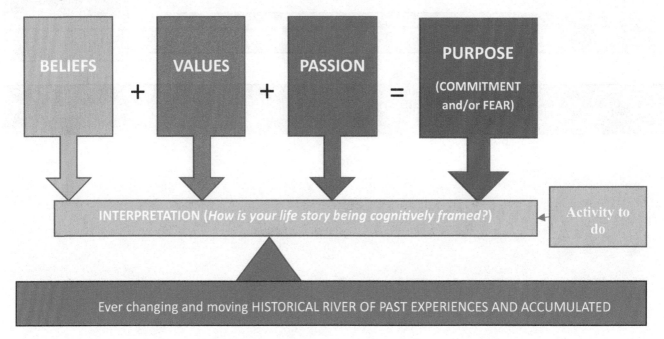

The question that might impact our *gap analysis* work more than any of the others mentioned, however, might be, "How would you get to know someone's *belief, value, passion* and *purpose* (*commitment and/or fear*)?"

As we move forward to work through the above words (which carry so much meaning … depending on your own mindset), let me start by saying I am purposefully drawing a distinct difference between them. As I do this work with large groups, it is interesting how many in the group interpret these terms differently. The nuances between these terms can make the defining of them (and subsequently the use of them) daunting. The main point of this book is centered around these four red boxes. How valuable would it be to be able to conduct a team member's annual review and have a reasonable way to knowing their core *belief,* their primary *value,* their deeper understanding of their *passion,* what they aim for in their *purpose/commitment* of life and, even more importantly, what they *fear*? Why is the *fear* component so important? The answers to these questions are the major takeaways of this book.

BELIEFS

Let's start with the word *belief*. Typically, when we use this word, we must be careful in an organization because of the religious overtones of the word. But not all beliefs are faith-based or fall into the arena of religion. How I am using the term for this work centers on the fact that we all have convictions or thoughts that we are convinced, have some level of truth in our minds. For this work, I am using the word as follows: A *belief* is a truth we hold onto even in the most uncertain times.

When I am working in the educational industry, I will ask a group of educators what is a *belief* most in education believe or should believe? They almost always say, "*All students can learn.*" That is or should be, a universal *belief* for all teachers. Most industries have these core tenants or convictions at the center of their work that would classify as a *belief*. Of course, some of our *beliefs* are much more common and/or noticeable, while others are deeper and are hidden deeper in our mindsets.

One of the *beliefs* my mother taught me was that it is my responsibility to care for the poor. It was odd that she taught me that because I thought we were poor. But it was a *belief* she taught me. She even told me she was going to check up on me later in life to see if I followed through. She would kid, "*When you get older, I am going to come and look at your checkbook to see if you are caring for the poor!*" (If you knew my mom, you would know she wasn't kidding.) On the other hand, my dad obviously taught me a *belief* that hard work pays off. If you didn't work hard, he would *motivate* you to work hard. The military taught me that same *belief,* as well.

Before we move on, what are some of your core beliefs? What are some *interpretations* of your *thought river that* have produced in you some deeper-seeded truths that you hold to, even in the deepest hours of life?

Core Beliefs – What do you hold to be true at the root of your life?

The interesting thing about our *beliefs* is how they affect our every decision. We really don't make decisions contrary to our *beliefs*. Yet, it is equally interesting how hard it is for most readers of this book to even complete the above task. The one I just asked you to complete. Did you write anything in the box? Or did you simply keep reading? During one-on-one coaching sessions with clients, I have found that the identification of core beliefs is work that is amazingly simple to consider but incredibly hard to do. Most of us talk about the fact that we have core beliefs (again, outside the arena of faith), but we are typically not able to quickly identify them. We are often not as reflective as we could be or should be.

VALUES

Before we say more about the area of *beliefs*, let's move into the area of *values*. This again begs the question about definitions. What is the difference between a *belief* and a *value?* Again, when doing this work with groups, at times, I hear those in the group define these two terms interchangeably. I would not pretend to have the corner on all the etymology of this word, *value*, but if you do the research on it, you will eventually read how I would like to use it for this book: A *value* is a standard of weight or importance we put on one thing over the other. Some things in our lives have more value than other things. Two things can have value, but they don't always, or even seldom, hold the same value to us. For instance, we might value our family, and we might value our work (occupation). But we seldom value them the same. How I really want to use this term is to say that *values* are the weight we put on one *belief* over the other. We might have several *beliefs*. But we also typically *value* one of those *beliefs* more than the others. Let me illustrate this thought using the above beliefs that were imprinted in my life by my mom and my dad.

About three miles from my home is a Starbucks. To say I am obsessed with Starbucks is to know me. I have written all my books at a Starbucks location, and I am currently sitting in one as I write this section. Recently, during my daily afternoon trip to Starbucks, I stopped at the end of the exit ramp and to my right was my favorite Starbucks. I had ordered ahead, and a tall cold drink after a long, tough day was waiting for me. To the left of me, at the stop sign, there was a person standing holding a sign. He obviously had an *activity* he wanted me to do. He wanted money for food. He wanted a quick *transaction*. He didn't know about my *thought river* at all. He probably didn't care about MY *thought river*, actually! He simply had a need, and this was his method to fill that need.

What he didn't know was my interpretation of my life story was making it difficult for me to simply respond and/or engage in his requested *transaction* activity. The issue I faced (that he was not aware of it) was which one of my core beliefs would take over in this situation. Would my mother's voice of *care for the poor* come shining through, motivating me to give him money? Or would my dad's shouting out to me, *work hard,* muzzle my mom's words? Would I roll down the window and give him money, or yell at him, *get a job*!? What he also didn't know was that I had another truth (*belief*) in my

thought river. That *belief* was that *David needs to reward himself every day with a frappe from Starbucks.* Which *belief* will win out? (Stay tuned!)

The challenge we face with our *values* is how we determine which one, at times, we want to hold to above the other. Let's consider education again. Prior to March 2020 (Covid-19), what do you think most educators *valued*? They, of course, *valued* pedagogy, AND they *valued* the safety of their students. Yet, if you looked at the way they used their time and money, you would draw the conclusion that (prior to Covid-19) they *valued* pedagogy over safety. (By the way, we can often see what a person *values* by how they spend their money and their time … hence, my mom wanting to see my checkbook).

After March 2020, however, what did we see education *value*? They obviously put greater value on safety over pedagogy since they sent all the students home. It was NOT that they didn't *value* pedagogy (contrary to the *belief* of some). It was just that a worldwide pandemic took away their primary and only known way to do pedagogy. (Can you see the *cognitive anchor* in that statement?) Leaders in education had to make a very difficult decision about which *value* they were going to use to make those decisions. They still believed in the truth that *all students can learn*. However, they also have the *belief* that students should be safe. Suddenly both *beliefs* were in competition with each other and created a competing *values* framework for each of them. Most of what we now see in school boards, and parent engagement regarding their children's education is a competing *value* framework model. (The *cognitive corral* we live in determines our mindset about this strain impacting education.)

There is much more we can discover when comparing *beliefs* and *values*. However, let's stop and consider how specifically these two areas fit into our *gap analysis* work. How important is knowing a person's deeper *beliefs* and how they *value* one over the other when considering someone for a new position within the organization? How important is knowing their *belief* and *value* when conducting their yearly review? Typically, when we consider *value* work, we do it separate from *belief* work. Or we wrongly merge the two words into one meaning, drawing no distinction between the two. We also tend to give people lists of general vanilla *values* to choose from. During in-take questions for the beginning of one-on-one coaching sessions, I will ask a new client to list for me their top three to five values by which they truly live. After hundreds and hundreds of those sessions, I can tell you I seldom find anyone who just rattles off the core *values* they live by. But if I give them a list, they can pick the *values* that sound good to them. There is certainly nothing wrong with a list of *values* from which to choose. But if I *value* caring over hard work, it matters. At least to the guy holding the sign. Do you know what you value? What are your top three to five values?

Values – What do you give your highest priority to in life?

(Hint: Look at your check book, credit card statement, and/or your calendar appointments)

1. Value #1 –

2. Value #2 –

3. Value #3 –

4. Value #4 –

5. Value #5 –

Passion

Sticking with our trend, how would you define *passion* regarding this work? What is the difference between *passion, values*, and/or *beliefs*? Let's say it this way:

Belief is a conviction we hold true even in the most critical moments of life.

Value is the weight of importance and/or priority of all our collective *beliefs*.

Passion is the energy we feel, demonstrate, and/or express as we are living out our *beliefs* and *values*.

Passion is what others see, and we feel. It is an amazing energy that comes over us when we are talking, walking, behaving and/or simply living in our favorite spot, moment, time of our life journey.

PASSION

When you use a thesaurus to look for synonyms to *passion*, you will read *devotion*, *enthusiasm*, and *affection*. Antonyms are *hatred, antagonism, and hostility*.

So, one effective way to think of *passion* is to think of it as doing something you love energizes you. This is so important to our work on *gap analysis*.

Knowing what a person is *passionate* about is vital to knowing how they will fit into the culture of the organization or your department and/or mingle with their team members. If we were to say that our *beliefs* are the map of our lives and our *values* are our compass, then our *passions* would be the fuel of our souls.

If we put people into the wrong place in the organization, department, and/or team, and it drains them of their *passion*, we have done them (and us) a severe disservice. It is, however, amazing how many people will take a job just for compensation and/or security and not because it is their *passion*. That would be sad if it were not for the fact that it is even more dangerous. We can't expect every part of our occupations to give us *passion* or to even feed our *passion*. But if we are not experiencing the energy that our *passion* can supply us most of our day, we ought to wake up and consider where we are or what we are doing.

It might be helpful in our explanation of *passion* to take time to explain the color scheme of our diagram on page 11, the light red, to a dark red color system, regarding *beliefs, values, passions,* etc. If you noticed, when we arrived at *passion,* I used an opening sentence to say that *passion* is what others *see*. This is the first time we talked about something in our mindset that others *see* or *observe*. The colors move from light red to darker red, left to right, because I am trying to communicate that *beliefs* are very much internal. When expressed, *values* begin to come out of us, and others can start to see them as we make our daily priority choices. When we get to *passion,* others start to *see* what ignites and pleases us, and we can see in others what they are *passionate* about. You can see this when you give a team member a task that they really enjoy. Their energy level grows, and it is almost always contagious. The converse, however, is also true. When our daily tasks take us to areas we do not enjoy, we lose energy. That can also be highly contagious. Later, as we get to *purpose (commitment)* in our diagram, we see that box in my diagram is a much darker red. The more we manifest our *passion* via our *purpose* and/or *commitment*, we allow others to really see who we are. We will cover more of this as we reach the end of our diagram, but the takeaway element is that our mindset does have a visible and tangible outpouring (though it is unseen and composed of an internal complicated structure of neurons). Just as a river pours into an ocean, so, too, our *thought river* will pour out into our lives in visible actions. Others will observe and gaze at our behavior(s). Yet what they see first started as a simple thought that ended as a tangible action.

Passion is a great outcome of our *thought river*. All our accumulated experiences and knowledge produces this thing (can I really call it a *thing*) that acts like a fire in our soul. People spend a lot of money to find their *passion*, to pursue their *passion*, and/or protect their *passion*. There are plenty of life coaches and leadership coaches who help others discover their *passion*. When I had my heart attack at 55, I came to the realization that I was doing activities each day that did not get me anywhere near my *passion* world. I finally had to stop what I was doing and bring my *beliefs* and *values* into alignment with my *passion*. But I had a serious problem. In all those years, I have *never* spent any time identifying or defining, with intentionality, my *passion*.

I was 55, and I could not say aloud what it was that really gave me consistent, unbridled energy. I knew when I was energized, but I didn't know how that happened. Others could see me when I was naturally energized, but they didn't know why I was. I started to refer to this aspect of my life as my *unwritten, unpublished normative* of life. What I meant by this statement was that I realized I had never taken the time to *write* out my most *normative* desire (*unwritten*). I had never taken the time to talk to anyone about what it was that gave me energy (*unpublished*). I had never taken the time to process it with anyone. It was a *normative* because when I am engaged in it, that is, when I feel the most natural (*normal* or *healthy*?). When I ask others what they believe their *unwritten, unpublished normative* might be, they just stare at me. And rightly, they should. Who asks questions like that using terms like that? But now that you know a bit about what an *unwritten, unpublished normative*, what would you write for your *passion* statement:

Passion Statement – What is your *unwritten, unpublished normative* of life?

(What is driving the internal emotion that gives you energy?)

My *passion* statement is up on my office wall in vinyl letters. It reads as follows:

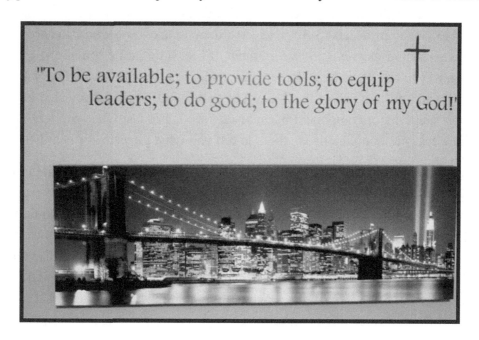

My *passion* is to do what I am doing right now. I am writing a book that can be used as a tool to equip leaders. I am developing a tool that will not just equip them but enable them to do good. This, I believe, brings glory to my God. I get a complete tank full of energy writing. I get a tank full of energy speaking to groups. However, I get more energy from one-on-one coaching sessions. That is where real work is done, and those I coach are *equipped*.

A key in *gap analysis* is helping others identify their own *passion*. If you are struggling with what to write in the above box, let me give you a small but significant exercise to start the intentional process of identifying your *passion*; your *unwritten, unpublished normative*. This is a three-step process:

Step #1 - For the next 3-4 weeks, before you start your morning, take ten minutes of very quiet, intentional time to look at your day. These ten minutes should not be part of your driving to work time, or you're getting ready for the day, time, or part of a multi-tasking activity. This is intentional, reflective time set aside to do this work. Look at the meetings, calendar dates and events before you for the day and rank them on a scale from 1-10. If you think the activity, meeting or event is going to give you energy, rank it #10. If you think, however, that the event is going to suck the energy out of your very bones, rank it #1. The hope is that you will, with intentionality, recognize what you *think* will give you energy. What *might* be in your *passion* wheelhouse? After you do this, simply go through your day.

Step #2 – In the evening, you can reflect on step #1 if you would like, but that is not the only exercise you should do in the evening. Again, with ten minutes of quiet reflection time (good luck if you have small children in your home or a needy spouse), look back over your day and finish this statement: Today *I received the most energy from* _____. The point of this step is to recognize when you did something that gave you energy (whether scheduled or random). In this step, you are intentionally taking note of it in your life. (Clients who complete this activity often tell me that what they record in Step #2 was not even on their daily schedule in Step #1.)

Step #3 – Solicit one or two people who really know you and see you on a regular basis to help you. It is best to have one person at work and one who sees you at home or out of work, if possible. Ask them to watch you and listen to you over the next 3-4 weeks. Ask them to take note when you are super excited, full of energy, and demonstrating a most *passionate* moment of life. It might be something they saw you doing or something they heard you telling them. Ask them not to tell you when they see it or hear it from you. Ask them to record it and wait until the end of the 3-4 weeks to tell you. This is a key step to this activity. The observations of others are a major component because *passion* is not just what you feel, but it is also what others see. After the weeks are completed, ask them to tell you what they saw or heard.

At the end of these three steps, you will have a self-assessment of what you anticipated would give you energy, what you observed gave you energy and what others noticed gave you energy. This activity is a key element in this work of *gap analysis*. It is simple, yet if you are intentionally looking for what gives you energy (and having others look for it), you will see some unique patterns. This allows you, with extreme intentionality, to identify areas of your life that are in your *passion* world. I will tell you that I have had clients who did this exercise and discovered when it comes to their work or professional life, they see very little. I tell them that after the first week, if they have nothing that they can identify that gives them passion in steps #1 and #2, call me immediately. That is harder for you, the reader of a book. But it does say something if you anticipated something giving you energy, and it didn't deliver. There are many reasons for that, but it should be a caution flag for us when we anticipate the energy, and it doesn't deliver. It is a red flag if you go for a significant time and have few, if any, of your daily activities energize you.

If we can't find our *passion*, have we not just identified a *gap*? The *gap* between our *passion* and your work might be one of the most important to identify.

Often this activity, however, supplies great clarity for those who do it diligently. They are amazed at what they observe, and others observe in them regarding their *passion*. They begin to see patterns and activities that are rooted in the same place or similar places. This is what you are looking for. If you have someone process this with you, they might see areas you are not able to see. An outside set of eyes can often give you more to look at than your own eyes can see.

It should be noted that even after we identify our *passion*, we know that our entire day does not always align or center on what we discovered. However, we must identify the *passion* before we can actually find a possible *gap* between our *passion* and our day-to-day activities. Our *thought river* is churning and moving every day. It takes our *beliefs*, our *values* and our *passion*s and produces in our lives an amazing story. *Gap analysis* is about finding out where the thought river of your mindset does not match and align with your day-to-day work world. Organizations also have stories. They have *beliefs*, *values* and *passions* (often, they refer to the latter as their *mission* statement). We can't do any *gap analysis* work if we don't identify these areas for both the organization and those who lead and follow in the organization.

Before we move on to the last red box in our diagram, let me give you another tool that might help regarding what is a normal, misalignment of your day-to-day with your thought river passion. Even those who work for themselves and have no one overseeing them can't live in their passion world all the time, every day. I found this to be one of the most concerning issues coming out of my past heart attack. I started to identify what parts of my day-to-day journey gave me energy and what parts did not. I, of course, knew what to do with the areas that gave me energy; I needed to keep doing those activities! But what about all those activities that I was responsible for but did not give me energy and did not feed my passion? That is when I created my personal bucket list. (I explain this bucket list in Addendum 1. I hope it will help you get closer and closer each day to your passion world and allow you to live in it all day long. That seldom can happen, but it won't happen for even a moment if you don't take some intentional steps to do that alignment work.)

PURPOSE (Commitment and/or Fear)

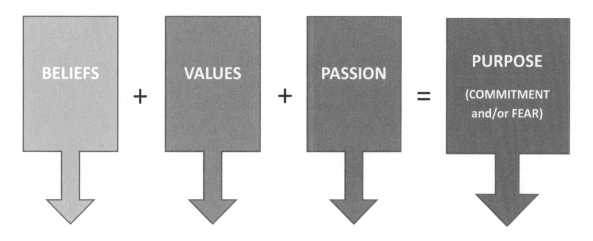

If you return to the mindset diagram on page 2, you will see that there are *plus* signs between the areas of *beliefs*, *values* and *passion* and then an *equal* sign prior to the *purpose* red box. See below:

Purpose (or *commitment*) is even more visible to those around us than our *passion*. It is the action step we take each day to carry out our *beliefs*, *values* and *passion*. This is what we do very visibly each day; that is the culmination of all the other parts of our *thought river*. The word *purpose* is extraordinarily strong in our lives. We live for a *purpose*. How you define your *purpose* determines most of your day-to-day actions. The reason I also like the word *commitment*, parenthetically inserted, is because it conveys an even deeper look into the *purpose* actions of our lives. Our *commitment* is what we are willing to do and what we do each day to fulfill our combined *beliefs, values* and *passions*. To me, it is the obligatory action I MUST take as a result of the other three. It is my *purpose*, yes. And I am absolutely *committed* to get that done! Most team members and/or leaders will not *commit* to something they don't *believe* in, *value* above all else, and does not align with what they are *passionate* about. This is a very visible part of our lives. If you ask me to do an *activity* and it aligns with my *belief*, my *values*, and my *passion*, it will soon become my *purpose*, something I am *committed* to doing each day. We are highly engaged when we are *committed* about something because it is our *purpose* for working (or, in some respects living). Our *purpose/commitment* is so important to us that we will protect it at all costs. Typically, we will not do anything that prevents us from reaching our *purpose* in life. This is why we use the word *fear* in this diagram. There is a strong relationship between what we are *committed* to, based upon our *purpose* and our *fear(s)*. Regarding this relationship, Dr. Robert Kegan has written extensively on this subject in his book (co-authored by Lisa Laskow Lahey), *Immunity to Change: How to Overcome It and Unlock the Potential in Yourself and Your Organization* (*Leadership for the Common Good*), published by *Harvard UP*, January 1, 2009. Part of the work the authors outline for us in *Immunity to Change* is that we *fear* anything we perceive might prevent us from accomplishing what we are committed to in life. Let's suppose that we are *committed* to going north in our work style. But we take a new job, and the entire new organization is *committed* to a south work style. We might *fear* the *activities* of this organization, or leadership, are asking us to do. If we perceive that these activities tell us to go south and will not allow us to go north, we will *fear* doing them. Our *north* in this illustration is what we have identified as a major *purpose/commitment* of our lives. So being told each day to go south causes us to understand that we can't, then, go north. But more importantly, we can't reach a major life *purpose* if we *fear* something we are being asked to do will hinder that *purpose*. We are going to revisit this in subsequent chapters. Suffice it to say, this is a major part of our *thought river*. We will go to great lengths to reach our *purpose* in life. The more conscious this *purpose/commitment* is to us, the more we can close the *gaps* when asked, required, and/or instructed to do something for our work responsibilities. Yet, if that ask, or requirement, or instruction goes contrary to our *purpose/commitment*, we might resist following through with it since we *fear* it will prevent us from reaching our *purpose/commitment* in life. This is truly where we begin to create a *gap* in our work product each day. When we see team members failing to follow through in these areas, we might put them on individual development plans (IDPs). However, the IDPs is almost always engage in more and more activities that go against their *purpose/commitment* for life. They will *fear* these IDP requirements even more than the original ask, requirement or instruction. (You would do well to invest in Dr. Kegan and Lisa Laskow Lahey's book for deeper study.)

Individualization

How is your story being behaviorally voiced? Let's move all this talk of *beliefs, values, passion* and *purpose/commitment* to the more practical side for our *gap analysis work*. How is your life, developed by your *cognitive framing*, playing out in your day-to-day *behavioral voice*? Let's finish off our diagram by looking at how we might characterize our *behavior* in a way that respects our life story, but that also gives us some insight into how we might *bridge the gaps* we can find between our story and the story of the organization. Note how our *thought river* produces our *beliefs, values, passions* and our *purpose*, and then that *cognitive framing* produces a *voice* we express in distinct behavior patterns. *Individualization* is a time-honored right. At least, that is what we would like to believe. If you doubt this thought, visit any home with a child in any one of the stages of adolescence. They desperately want to be their *own person*. They are fighting internal and external pressures to conform. However, they only desire their own *individual* way to live their lives. This eventually subsides as we enter adulthood (for most), but nevertheless, their journey is worthy to note. Many adult workers still struggle with the balance between their *individuality* and the requirement to conform to an organizational meaning. *Gap analysis* is a key to understanding this *gap* by understanding how the *individualization* is voiced and formatted by their *thought river*. Here is where work-life meets *individualization* and the *ever-changing and moving historical river of past experiences and accumulated knowledge*. When we attempt to *bridge the gap* between what we need in our organization and what we hire in this *individualization* framework, we can feel highly disrespected and a forced need to conform. Sometimes this is done for the sole purpose of conformity. Here is where we must ask the question as to whether we retain and hire staff that aligns with our *values*. If you want to cause a commotion in the workplace, hire, retain, and or promote staff who do not align with your *values*. Wait...is that true? Do we retain, promote, and hire ONLY those who share our *values*? Or do we retain, promote and hire team members with different, diverse *beliefs* and *values*? There may be no *correct* answer to that question. I would prefer to answer it this way, which honors a person's life story and the *individualization* of that story: The more mature the organization, the more they can hire team members with different and even competing values. A less mature organization will tend to need *compliance* to succeed. Mature organizations embrace diverse *beliefs* and *values* in the *behavioral voice*. If that premise is true, how do we hire team members with diverse *beliefs, values, passions,* and *purpose/commitments* and still assure that *individualization* does not become disruptive to the organizational goals, missions and desired outcomes? Perhaps one way to change the paradigm is to replace the thought of someone having to *share our core values* in order to work here with the thought that team members must *align with our values* to work here, but only while they work here! That is a slight difference in a statement that carries a wide divergence of outcomes. If we make people conform to the organizational *belief* and *values,* they might perceive we are jeopardizing or threatening their individuality. If, however, we require them to align with the organization's *beliefs* and *values*, we can both honor their individualization and maintain organizational fidelity.

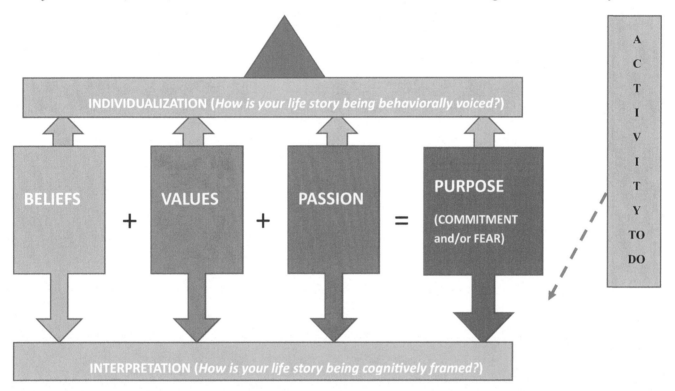

If you and I must meet at a certain time, on a certain day, to do certain work, we both need to align to the *value* of punctuality. I personally may not be an "*on-time-for-events* person", however. I may practice my life by showing up when I want. Or, perhaps, that is your lifestyle, as well. But, for the purpose of this meeting, we must *align around the value* of being punctual. We don't have to change who we are as *individuals*, but we must agree to *align our values* for the work we agree to do.

Conforming individuals to our organization should not be the goal of a hiring process. We are not attempting to conform people to our desired model. That is not only short-cited but also disrespectful. Whenever we hire, retain, and promote, we ought to be looking for individuals who will bring their *individuality*, which flows from their *thought river* of life, but who also agree to *align* with our organizational *beliefs and values* for the time they are working with us and for us.

As we move forward into Part 2, we will unfold how we create this alignment between individuals and organizations for the purpose of *bridging the gaps*. But, before we do this work, we must stop and consider some ways to describe this *individualism*. We need some common language to understand how we align *individualism* (caused by this *thought river*) to our organizational culture. This will allow us to conduct our *gap analysis* and *bridge the gaps* that need a bridge. For this reason, let's unfold the wonder and power of *archetypal imprints* and language.

PART 2

Understanding How Our Archetypal Stories Impact and Express Our Mindset

What's in the well comes up in the bucket.

(David's first law of life!)

When we are attempting to identify our life pathways, journey, or patterns of behavior, there may be no greater method than to understand our *archetypal imprints* of life. If you have never studied *archetypes,* this chapter will close a *gap* for you. If you have done work centered around *archetypal language,* you can move quickly to the last half of Part 2. In this first section, we are simply going to take time to introduce you to *archetypes.* Here is Webster's definition of archetype:

Webster defines the word as follows:

Archetype comes from the Greek verb *archein* ("to begin" or "to rule") and the noun *typos* ("type"). *Archetype* has specific uses in the fields of philosophy and psychology. The ancient Greek philosopher Plato, for example, believed that all things have ideal forms (aka archetypes) of which real things are merely shadows or copies. And in the psychology of C. G. Jung, *archetype* refers to an inherited idea or mode of thought that is present in the unconscious of the individual. In everyday prose, however, *archetype* is most used to mean "a perfect example of something."

To me, archetypes are the beginning imprints of your life. If you have children and you are trying to form them into what you hope they will become, you are *imprinting* them. As they grow older and people say they act more and more like you, you can say they are the archetype of you. They are an *example of you.* Maybe not a *perfect* example, but an example. In fact, most teachers have a better understanding of their students after a parent-teacher conference. Do you get it?

When trying to understand the world of *archetypes,* it is essential to remember the last part of Webster's definition: *"Archetypes are a perfect example of something."* It might be ill-advised to use the word *perfect* with anything, but let's just roll with it. What we are observing in an *archetypal* language is an excellent way to define patterns of behavior in a collective manner that gives a tool for our *gap analysis* work.

It should first be noted that there are hundreds of *archetypal* imprints. If you hear someone say, "Great grandpa," what do you think of? If you had a relationship with your great-grandfather, you might have some references to consider. If you didn't know your great-grandfather or even your grandfather, you might not have a real reference for this archetypal term. Yes, *great-grandfather* is an archetypal term. Why? It gives us a pattern or example of a pattern of behavior. It is a way to describe a particular way of life.

If I say *mother,* or *police officer,* or *marine,* or *politician,* or *teacher,* it conjures up in our minds all types of behavioral patterns. Archetypal patterns are used to describe characters in books. A good character in a novel has a primary archetypal behavior that we can wrap our brains around. The *hero* is an archetypal imprint. As is the *villain.*

We can certainly look at archetypes through the lens of psychology, but that really limits our understanding. Archetype patterns are used by marketing firms to sell products to a certain archetypal audience. To sell golf clubs or any athletic product, you want to have someone who fits the athletic brand to ensure your marketing campaign is going to be the most effective. Using a television ad campaign as an example, you would fare better selling athletic wear during an athletic event than you would during a Hallmark movie. The same is true for any product.

Archetypal behavior gives us an avenue to identify how people think or might respond. We should be using archetypal language for our hiring process (more on this in Part 4). Let's assume you want someone for your new receptionist position. How would you describe this would be a team member? Use the box below to write out your description for this job positing:

How you describe the person will be based upon the archetypal language of your mindset. You probably described a person with an outgoing personality. You might have said you want the candidate to be organized. Perhaps you stated you want them to be good at making quick judgments (think on their feet) and be a good problem solver. Maybe you said they must have a lot of energy, and you want them to have a deep desire to care for and be helpful. The above is a description of a particular archetypal imprint. This imprint can be defined in specific archetypal terms. That is what this section is about.

How would you describe the best candidate for your new receptionist position?

PART 2a
12 Archetypes Described (The possible stories of our mindsets)

Starting this section, let me state that if you are familiar with the archetypes, this section could be redundant. In my previous three books, I have supplied my thoughts on twelve archetypal stories. If you have a good understanding of the archetypes, you can skip to Part 2b. We are going to use this material here in Part 2a when we move into Part 2b. In that section, we will be merging our mindset diagram from page 2 to these 12 archetypal stories.

If you don't understand the archetypes, I will use the next section to either introduce or reacquaint you with them, as well as equip you with some practical tools. Regardless of your prior understanding, for anyone who would like to dive deeper into the archetypes, let me also suggest some additional resources:

1.   I have already written three books on archetypes, *Just Middle Manager* and *Archetypes and the Drama of Change* (published by The Book Publishing Pros) and *TRUST! Using Archetypal Language to Rebuild Broken Trust* (The Book Publishing Pros).
   The first is a basic primer about twelve archetypes and how they relate to one's leadership style. The second deals with leading an institution through some change to its culture. The third uses the unique language archetypal imprints provide us as a tool to connect with others after trust has been broken. All titles provide a deeper understanding of how to use the archetypes in your leadership and organizations and can be ordered directly from my website: www.hulingsandassociates.com.

2.   Dr. Carol S. Pearson is considered by many to be the foremost expert on archetypes. Check out her website (www.carolspearson.com) for a wealth of excellent resources.

3.   Dr. Pearson also collaborated with Hugh K. Marr in the development of an inventory that will assess the activity of the archetypes. The Pearson-Marr Archetype Inventory (PMAI) ® is available at www.StoryWell.com. The StoryWell site is also a valuable resource for other archetype material, including additional authors to further deepen your knowledge base.

Basic Archetype Understanding

Before we unpack the twelve archetypes and apply them to our *mindset gap analysis* work, let me supply some insight to archetypes taken directly from my previous books. These guidelines and descriptors will enable you to grasp a better understanding of archetypes (or reacquaint you) and how powerful they are to our mindset.

1.   As stated earlier, the word archetypes simply means the beginning imprints of your life. We might better understand them as building blocks for the story of your life. Any parent understands the thought of imprints. We are constantly trying to imprint our children. We are trying to impress on them the behaviors and character qualities we want them to exhibit, whether they are with us or not with us. What parent has not puffed their chest out a little and lifted their chin a wee bit higher when they see their child mimic an imprint that the parent has worked so hard to impress into the heart, soul, and mind of said, child? But what parent has not also observed a very poor imprint from their child and not pointed to their spouse, stating: "*We all know where that comes from!*" These imprints are not just established in our childhood, however. We can have a college professor, a first boss, or any other significant person imprint us. Archetypes are a way to describe, categorize or tell a story.

2. As stated a few pages ago, there are many archetypes in the world. The Pearson-Marr Archetype Inventory (PMAI) ® measures someone on twelve representative archetypes, but there are many terms and descriptors that conjure up diverse types of thoughts in our minds. We must avoid believing that the twelve I am using in this work are the limits to archetypal discovery. These twelve indeed help us, but they cannot cage our thinking on archetypes.

3. Archetypes have a strength side and a shadow side. Think about a tree that has the sun to the south. The south side of the tree would always have the sun. This is a big tree. It has many limbs. It has birds in its limbs. It has a treehouse in the limbs. It is a big tree. On the south side, you would always have that sun. For this metaphor, we will call that south side the strength side of the tree. On the north side of the tree, you would always have a shadow. It would be cooler, but there would also be moss growing on this side. It might even have other things that like to grow and live in dark and dingy places. For our metaphor, we will call this the shadow side of the tree. If you have the strength side, you also have the shadow side. The only way you would remove the shadow side of the tree is to cut off the limbs. If you cut off the limbs, you would eliminate the shadow side of the tree, but you would also lose the limbs, the fruit, the treehouse, and probably the birds. You would be left with the stump. I have been hired, on far too many occasions, to fix or repair someone's shadow side. The shadow side is not something we fix. It could be referred to as the Achilles Heel. It is as natural as the shady side of that tree. There are some difficult looks the shadow side of an archetype presents, to be sure. But those are

4. Simply what comes with the strength side of the archetype. More about this as we unfold Part 2b and Part 3.

5. We tend to view the archetypes we like only in their strength form, but the archetypes we don't like only in their shadow form. The word *like* is probably a weak word for that thought. It might be healthier to state when we see an archetype in the lives of others that are also active in our life, we tend to view that archetype in its strength form. But, when we see an archetype in the lives of others that we are less familiar with or are not active in our lives, we tend to view that archetype in a shadowy manner. This, of course, is not healthy for leaders or followers; nevertheless, it is most true than not. Perhaps this is where we get the concept of first impressions. The antidote for this challenge is to read more about the archetypes and understand them more fully. That can cause us to view them all in a strength manner and allow us to understand the natural shadow side we are going to see with that archetype.

6. The archetypes give us a wonderful way to understand human behavior, the structure of the mindset, unconscious bias, and/or adjust our behaviors. I believe that is especially true when it comes to our *beliefs, values, passions, purpose/commitment* and *fears* (more in Part 2b). Archetypes not only allow us to know *how* a person is acting (giving us a healthy and descriptive way to describe the how), but also (and more importantly) they can give us a glimpse into *why* a person acts the way they do. The importance of this thought cannot be understated. When trying to work through conflict and trust, we must be able to not just see how a person is acting during a conflict, but we must get deeper into the why. It is the *why* that determines our ability to name the catalyst, the fear, and the exact assurance we need to convey before we follow through.

7. Archetypes are prominent in many fields. We can use archetypes when describing how marketing directors sell products. Most television commercials can easily be described in archetypal language. The characters of a novel are developed in an archetypal manner. Sitcoms and Disney characters

reflect archetype imprints. Political campaigns often communicate in archetype themes. It is hard to find a place where you can't use archetypes to describe, understand or explain a pattern of behavior. This helps us in our work with *mindset gap analysis* as well. Those struggling with a *mindset gap* need to have a pathway out of that struggle. Using archetypal patterns to navigate possible *gaps* is natural to us.

8.   The archetypes are best understood in balancing pairs. The best way to unpack the depth of each archetype is to realize the concept that two different archetypes can help each other navigate life. If you think of them as one on each end of a teeter-totter, that gives you a good visual about how they should operate. You don't want to be off balance between two archetypes. If you have one archetype in the strength form on one side and the pair of that archetype in the shadow form, you have the ingredients for internal conflict (that often manifests itself in behavioral conflict). Below we will outline the twelve archetypes in Dr. Pearson's and Hugh Marr's PMAI®. They are better understood, however, as six pairs rather than twelve independent imprints. In Part 3, we will unpack these pairs to show us how to use them in solving areas of our *mindset gaps* we want to bridge.

9.   When describing archetypes, they are often associated with personality. The truth and accuracy of that association would depend on how you define personality. The word personality, in my work, is often what I refer to as a *junk drawer* word. Most people have a *junk drawer* in their homes. They don't, however, put *junk* into the drawer. They put stuff in the drawer that they simply don't have another place to put it. They don't put pots and pans in the drawer because they have a place for pots and pans. They don't put their fancy China in the drawer since they have a place for their fancy China. They put things in the drawer that have no place to go. That is like the word personality in our country. If we don't know what the behavior, action, or quality is in someone's life, we simply say, "That's just his/her personality." For many reasons, it doesn't matter how we associate archetypes with personality. The key thought to decide is if the archetypes are *us* or are *they* tools we have used to navigate the world around us. For this work, we will avoid the term personality and rather refer to the archetypes as *tools* we use to navigate our lives and tell the story of our lives. These imprints are powerful in how we live and move, and behave. For the work centered around *mindset gaps,* we will use these imprints to show us why we want to change something in our *gaps* but why we can't at the same time.

10.   When working with the thought that these archetypes are tools we use, it is important not to refer to another person as being an archetype. Many times, when these archetypes are presented to groups, attendees walk away saying things like, "*I learned today that I was a (enter archetype here)*!" Or "*I think you are a (enter archetype here)*!" When we are hoping to close a *mindset gap*, it is better if we view these as *tools* to use rather than using them to identify *how people are*. Rather than *lock* people in with a term, allow them to navigate to their own freedom with a *tool*.

11.   Since archetypes stem from the imprints of our lives, we can understand how they impact *beliefs, values, passions, purpose/commitments* and *fears*. Our imprints determine everything about us. They determine how we view the world and how we interpret the world. In the remainder of the book, we will see how they each impact our ability to identify and close *mindset gaps*.

12.   No one is just one archetype. That would be more of a stereotype. It is important to realize that people have many imprints in their river of life. A person can be quite familiar with more than one of the archetypes due to the many experiences they have had and the interactions they have had. We might want to think of archetypes like shoes in your closet. You decide the shoes you are going to wear based upon the activity and/or outfit for the day. You don't wear dress shoes to the beach, and you don't (shouldn't) wear flip-flops to a black-tie dinner. Some of the shoes you wear are super comfy. Others are tight, and you can't wait to get your feet out of them at the end of the

occasion. So, too, are archetypes. Think of these twelve archetypes as six pairs of archetypes in your leadership closet, like shoes. You are about to attend a meeting. What pair of archetypes should you wear for this meeting? It should be noted that you have some favorite archetypes (pair you like) that you use a lot. You have some that are less active in your day-to-day activities. You also, however, have some that are not even that conscious to you. Therefore, taking an assessment and looking at scores from an assessment ought to be done with some reservation and caution. For instance, there are some reasons you might score lower in an inventory on one archetype vs. another archetype. Here are some reasons to consider as to why you might score low on an archetype if you do take the PMAI® at www.storywell.com (I highly suggest you take it now if you have not done so).

a) ***Unfamiliar to you***. You might score low on an archetype if you have not had that imprint in your life. If you have no contact with an imprint, where would you get the imprint? It is foolish to think you would score high on something you have no conscious or unconscious imprint about. Yet, we are so obsessed with scores we don't like to see ourselves score low on something. ***Solution***: Learn about that imprint and teach yourself how to use it actively.

b) ***Uncomfortable to you***. You might be very familiar with an archetype, but in the past, when you used it in your life activities, something may have gone wrong. Perhaps you hurt someone by acting that way, and that causes you to no longer think of that *archetype* in a favorable manner. It is just uncomfortable for you when you are asked questions about it. ***Solution***: Relearn the archetype and learn where you used it in the shadow way and now want to use it in the strength manner.

c) ***Unfriendly to you***. You are familiar with it and comfortable using it, but you do not do well when someone uses it toward you or with you in some interaction. Perhaps you had a parent, or teacher, or coach, or friend, or ex-spouse that used the archetype in a shadowy way, and that turns you off when asked questions about it in an assessment. ***Solution***: Learn how to use the archetype in the strength way and how to deal with someone who is using it in the shadowy way.

d) ***Unneeded to you*** (at this time in your season of life). We go through seasons of life. Those seasons have a need for different archetypes to navigate that season. There are times when one archetype fits the time of your life, and another would not, and be a difficult tool to use that day. *Solution*: With intentionality, know the archetype and make sure you are using all discernment to make a conscious choice to not use it currently. However, ignorance that the archetype is not being used, but could be used, in not a wise choice.

e) ***Uncomplimentary to you***. Depending on the context, your home life, your work culture, your volunteer world, or your home community might need an archetype, or it might not. Perhaps you have a spouse or significant other who lives the archetype well and is displaying it actively in your world. You would allow them to use the archetype and not score it as active in your own life. Or the converse may be true. You could be working in a culture that does not value a particular archetype. If you demonstrated the activity of that archetype while at work, you might be less willing to score high on that archetype when asked questions about the activity of it in your life. *Solution*: Again, with intentionality, make sure that the archetype is being used by someone on the team, in the culture, in the home. If there is opposition to the archetype, the solution might be one of the reasons above.

f) ***Unable for you to use/practice***. You might work in an organization where a particular archetype is not used or valued. It is not just *uncomplimentary*. It is NOT ALLOWED. This is rare, but there are organizations that will simply tell you to not use a particular archetype behavior in their organization. This can cause a real *gap* between someone and the organization.

With these 11 points in our mindset, we can now look at the twelve archetypes we will use when we discuss the concept of *gap analysis*.

The Twelve Archetypes

Now that we have identified some basic observations about archetypes let's look at twelve that we are going to use for the rest of this work, how the archetypes work regarding our *mindset gap analysis*. To help the reader either become familiar with the archetypes the first time or a quick review, I offer the following chart, the *archetypes at-a-glance*. The chart is designed as follows:

Archetype's one-word descriptor	Strength Words	Shadow Words	What to do if work is piled up and must get done in one week	Today was a great day because…	Keywords/phrases they might use in an email
This is the one word used in the PMAI®. You will note that in the case of three of the archetypes, there are two terms used. The (descriptor) in parentheses is the old descriptor used in previous works by this author.	These are words that are often used to describe what the archetype might look like when the archetype is fully active in a <u>strength</u> manner. This is what we want the archetype to manifest when engaged in our lives.	These are the words that are often used to describe what the archetype might look like when the archetype is living in the <u>shadow</u> manner. This is not how we want the archetype to manifest when engaged in our lives.	This is what the archetype might look like if they arrive at work on Monday morning and the week's work is piled up to the ceiling, and the archetype has been told that all the work must be done by Friday afternoon. This is how the archetype would approach the work with their team in the <u>strength</u> manner. (How they respond to that situation can tell us a favorite go-to archetype.)	This material in this column will tell us how an archetype might finish the statement, "This was the best day ever at work because _____!" (How they finish that sentence can tell us their favorite or active archetype to live in each workday).	These are keywords the imprint of a particular archetype might create as a word bank for a particular archetype. This will become essential for when we talk about identifying and bridging *mindset* gaps, in the following sections of the book. The premise discussed here is that each archetypal imprint develops within our *mindset* a rich word bank that we draw upon whenever we speak or write or think.

Some dangers to consider:

1.   Using one word as a descriptor of any archetype is a dangerous game. An archetype cannot be reduced to one word. In the PMAI® inventory, there are six questions asked for each archetype. The six questions are measuring your response to an entire life behavior pattern. Reducing the archetypes to a one-word identifier is not always healthy. But the inventory is a wonderful place to start. It is not a tool to end the process. The PMAI® should be a starting point, not the finish line. This entire process should be the primer for an enjoyable conversation. It should not be a way to designate and categorize people.

2.   This at-a-glance chart provides an overview of the archetypes. It is simply a way to get the conversation going. It is not meant to be more than that.

Archetype's one-word descriptor	Strength Words	Shadow Words	What to do if work is piled up and must get done in one week	Today was a great day because …	Keywords/phrases they might use in an e-mail
Idealist (Innocent)	Optimism, Trust, Hope, Faith in All, Simple Virtue	Naiveté, Denial, Oblivious, Childlike, Toxic Positivity	Week's Work Offer hope that the job will get done; might lack REAL substance.	End-of-Day …because everything worked out just as I said it would.	Hoping, We can trust ____! It will all work out! Looking forward to …, Did I miss something? Don't worry about it!
Realist (Orphan)	Realism, Alertness, Independent, Empathy, Seldom Blindsided	Cynicism, Victimize, Complaining, Overly Critical	Week's Work Will point out dangers for the week; "I told you this was going to happen!"	End-of-Day …because I survived, rescued others and self from peril.	I doubt …, My worry is …, I don't trust ____! I am warning you all. That idea is flawed!
Warrior	Discipline, Courage, Determined, Skill	Arrogance, Ruthlessness, Fear of Losing Power	Week's Work Roll up their sleeves and get to work; might bark orders at everyone else.	End-of-Day …because I won! Was victorious and received the reward.	Excellence, Best, Crush, Win, I have your back! Let me step in!
Caregiver	Community, Nurturing, Compassion, Generosity	Enabling, Martyrdom, Guilt Motivated	Week's Work Let me help you all; I'll do your job … after I order pizza for all.	End-of-Day …because I served others sacrificially, helping them on their way.	Help, Support, Provide, What do you need? If you are busy, I can … I'm here if you need …
Seeker	Autonomy, Ambition, Wanderer, Possibility	Lack of Commitment, Alienation, Loneliness, Disappointment	Week's Work Let's use this time to find a new way to work; might never get THIS work done	End-of-Day …because I found a new idea beyond society's norms.	I'm looking for …, I discovered …, Let's see where we go …, Search, Could we consider …, That sounds promising!
Lover	Passion, Commitment, Enthusiasm, Enmeshment, Love Cures All	Overly Sensual, Objectifying Others, Entanglement	Week's Work "Let's make this a team effort;" might want to do work the same old way.	End-of-Day …because I was able to hold onto something or someone I love.	I love that! I like our approach! Hold, Embrace, Tradition, Remember, Last (week, year, etc.)

Revolutionary (Destroyer)	Metamorphous, Revolutionary, Capacity to Let Go	Hurting Others, Out of Control Anger, Harming Self	**Week's Work** Will calculate what should and shouldn't get done; but might toss good things away.	**End-of-Day** ...because I let go of something destructive, didn't waste time.	Let's take that down! It's broken! That failed! Can we move on! Wasting our time on …, Let it go! Makes no sense!
Creator	Inventive, Imaginative, Resourceful, Visionary	Self-Indulgence, Overwhelmed, Prima-Donna, Self-Governed	**Week's Work** Will create a new way to do things but might take too long to create the new way and miss the deadline.	**End-of-Day** ...because I created something new to better do old things.	Let's make _____! That's creative! It should look like this! Material, Construct, Plans, Nice idea, can I make it work?
Ruler	Responsible, In Control, Sovereign, System Person	Rigidity, Over-Controlling, Limited Vision, Entitlement	**Week's Work** Will assign tasks to everyone; might overly structure. (NO ruler would have seen this coming.)	**End-of-Day** ...because I put the kingdom in order (even if others don't know it).	Order, System, Policy and/or Procedure, Structure, Laws, What do the rules say?
Magician	Transformer, Catalyst for Change, Healer	Manipulation of others, Cultist Guru, Lack Reality, Kool-Aid Approach	**Week's Work** Will use the work to change attitudes; lack structure or methods.	**End-of-Day** ...because I transformed someone or something to reach their potential.	Let's change that! Fix, Transform, Change your mind! Think differently! My intuition says …, This could look like this …

Sage	Wisdom, Knowledge, Healthy Skeptic	Overly Critical, Pomposity, Impractical, Lack Empathy for Others	<u>Week's Work</u> Display historical, intellectual resources to fix problems; might not be practical today.	<u>End-of-Day</u> ...because I was able to learn something new and taught it to others.	I know …, Thought or Think, Interesting thought! That's deep! Understand, Gravitas, Alacrity
Jester	Humor, Living in the Moment, Joyous Light-Hearted	Irresponsible, Insensitive, Humor, Sloth, Con Artist	<u>Week's Work</u> Turn the project into a party; might be so relaxed quality control fails.	<u>End-of-Day</u> ...because I had a great time and made others laugh and enjoy their work.	I was just joking! That sounds fun! Enjoy, Laugh, Relax, Don't be so serious! Party, That was boring! That made me laugh! Great times!

Ten Archetype Exercises

Here are some good exercises to do with the at-a-glance chart. Working through these exercises will prepare you for the work presented in the remainder of this book:

Exercise One – Describing Archetypes

Using just the strength and shadow words of an archetype, how would you describe someone who has the following as the top archetypes of their lives (the most active) in a strength manner and a shadow manner?

Here is an example of how someone might be described with these three active archetypes:		
	How would they/could be described in a strength manner:	How would they/could be described in a shadow manner:
1. Warrior 2. Caregiver 3. Magician	This is a person who wants to excel in all they do, using their servant spirit to create transformation!	This is a person who could manipulate and enable others to get things done they want; they want it done!
What three would you select? **(If you took the inventory, use your top three. If you did not take it, go back and look at the at-a-glance material and select three that resonate with your life story. Remember, these are only a *start* to these conversations, however.)**		
1. 2. 3.		

Exercise Two – Ranking the Archetypes

If you take the PMAI® at www.storywell.com, this next exercise will be done for you. However, it might help you to do it here, first, or as well. Look at the at-a-glance chart and rank the archetypes in order of those that you think are the most active in your life now (#1) and the one that is the least active in your life right now (#12)

Ranking	Archetype	Where have you seen the archetype recently active in your life? Can you think of a moment in your life where the archetype could be used to describe that moment?
#1		
#2		
#3		
#4		
#5		
#6		
#7		
#8		
#9		
#10		
#11		
#12		

Exercise Three – The Archetype Pairs

Remember, the archetypes are best viewed in their pairs. Go back and look at the at-a-glance chart again. This time notice the pairs. Think about how one balances the other. What would life look like if each pair was in balance with the other? Go back to exercise #2 and record where you ranked the pairs:

The Archetype Pairs	How you ranked them in exercise #2	What is your reflection about each pair's balance?
Idealist (Innocent)		
Realist (Orphan)		
Warrior		
Caregiver		
Seeker		
Lover		
Revolutionary (Destroyer)		
Creator		
Ruler		
Magician		
Sage		
Jester		

Exercise Four – Creating the Story Behind the Archetypes

As stated earlier, archetypes can give us an understanding of behavior but also reveal the *why* behind what we do. This next exercise will help us identify some *whys* behind what might cause an archetypal behavior. Using only the descriptors as a clue, let's use our imaginations and try to identify a story in the past life of each archetype.

Perhaps, by now, you have started to identify some of your own stories or even stories of those you work with, for, and lead. This is not an easy task for some. If I asked my wife to do this type of exercise, she would probably say, "*Don't ask me to do that!*" She would say she scores low in imagination and creativity (the Creator archetype). But the value of exercise is very vital for us to understand how our past can imprint our lives and cause the archetypes to be manifested in our lives and identify any possible *gaps*. This is vital for later as we attempt to identify each archetype's *belief, value, passion, purpose/commitment* and *fear*. Using the form below, try to identify a story for each of the archetypes. This is your chance to expand your imagination. I will add my thoughts in the context for each archetype of how that archetype might have been rewarded in the past. People who have been rewarded for a behavior often desire to repeat that behavior with the hope they will be rewarded again and again. Use the at-a-glance chart to assist you in your work.

Archetype	Possible Story (Think of a real, specific story for yourself)	My Thoughts
Idealist (Innocent)		At an early age, they were told and rewarded for being positive and always looking on the bright side.
Realist (Orphan)		They once pointed out a danger that rescued or saved someone from harm. It gave them an instant high.
Warrior		They were rewarded for a competitive spirit or rewarded for performance.
Caregiver		They saw someone else helping others, and that person was rewarded for it. They, too, wanted that reward, so they copied that behavior (like from a parent).

Seeker		They were told multiple times they should find other ways to do something and were rewarded when they found a new way.
Lover		They were raised in a close-knit family that celebrated many traditions. They were rewarded for continuing those traditions and/or relationships.
Revolutionary (Destroyer)		They were told multiple times to not waste time on behaviors that were not profitable. They were rewarded for letting go of things, processes, and/or even people.
Creator		They were rewarded for their ability to create what their imaginations thought. When they put their imaginative ideas toward tangible things, they were rewarded.
Ruler		They were raised with a very tight and, perhaps, even rigid structure. Following the structure produced good things. Rebelling against the structure produced bad things in their life.
Magician		They had some event in their life that caused them to see the power of changing something. They watched the power of transformation and wanted that for themselves and others.

		Learning was rewarded. Knowing was rewarded. Research was rewarded. Data was rewarded. Education was a predominant feature in their lives.
Sage		
Jester		Fun was the most important aspect of their life. Being serious about life was downplayed. Making someone laugh brought instant reward. Embracing the moment brought them joy.

Exercise Five – The Archetype Drops a Child Off at Soccer Tryouts

This next exercise will continue to prepare us for *mindset gap analysis.* Using the last column in the at-a-glance chart, let's create some sentences that each archetype might use to describe an event. I will provide the event; you create the sentence. These can be either a strength or a shadow statement. Use the at-a-glance chart to help you in your work.

Here is the event: *Let's pretend the archetype is a parent. The parent is dropping their child off for the first day of varsity soccer tryouts. What would be the last sentence this parent (archetype) would say to their student-athlete to prepare them as they exited the car?*

Archetype	Your Sentence
Idealist (Innocent)	
Realist (Orphan)	
Warrior	
Caregiver	
Seeker	
Lover	

Revolutionary (Destroyer)	
Creator	
Ruler	
Magician	
Sage	
Jester	

Here are my suggested responses for this *archetypal* parent:

Archetype	Your Sentence
Idealist (Innocent)	It's going to be a great day. Don't worry about those tryouts. It will all work out.
Realist (Orphan)	Be careful. Especially be careful around that assistant coach. I think he's got your number.
Warrior	You worked all summer on conditioning/techniques. You'll ace the tryouts. We expect nothing less.
Caregiver	Try to help at practice. If the coach needs some help, volunteer. Make sure you make yourself available if the coach needs anything.
Seeker	Try something new at tryouts. Do something different. There is so much out there...Let the coach see you can do things differently than others.
Lover	Remember who you are today. Remember what we stand for in our family. Your team was so great last year you can make it like that this year. Make a friend today.
Revolutionary (Destroyer)	Forget about your last year's tryouts; that was last year. And quit hanging out with those loser friends. It's time to move on.
Creator	Offer to help the coaches with some of the projects during the season. Show them you can be valuable to the team in different ways. Tell the coach I am willing to create some new fundraisers.

Ruler	Listen to your coaches and do exactly what they say.
Magician	Make this day special. No matter what happens, it can be a wonderful day...Be willing to change if the coach asks you to change.
Sage	Learn something new today. Don't be afraid to offer to coach the other players and show them how to learn more.
Jester	Have fun …make someone laugh today. Get your team to have fun! Remember, it is only a game!

Exercise Six – The Archetypes and Famous Quotes

This exercise will also move us closer to using archetypes to identify *belief, value, passion, purpose/commitment* and *fear*. In the chart below, you will see the archetypes on the left side and a famous quote on the right side. Try to match the quote to the proper archetype. Use the at-a-glance chart to help you.

Archetype	Write in the column the best archetype voice that matches the quote	Quote
Idealist (Innocent)		Burn the boats!! Burn the boats!! (Or: That was yesterday's solution; let's move on.)
Realist (Orphan)		There is a place for everything, and everything should be in its place. (Or: It is my way or the highway.)
Warrior		Knowledge is power
Caregiver		The change you desire lies within you.
Seeker		Sleep with one eye open … you never know what is out there.
Lover		Find a job you enjoy, and you will never have to work a day in your life.
Revolutionary (Destroyer)		Anything worth doing is worth doing right, to the best of your ability. (Or: The easiest day you are going to have was yesterday)
Creator		Necessity is the mother of all invention.
Ruler		Boldly go where no man has gone before.
Magician		Don't worry, be happy … the sun will come out tomorrow.
Sage		Group Hug!! (Or: All you need is love!)
Jester		People don't care what you know until they know that you care.

My responses are on the next page:

Idealist (Innocent)	Revolutionary (Destroyer)	Burn the boats!! Burn the boats!! (Or: That was yesterday's solution, let's move on.)
Realist (Orphan)	Ruler	There is a place for everything, and everything should be in its place. (Or: It is my way or the highway.)
Warrior	Sage	Knowledge is power
Caregiver	Magician	The change you desire lies within you.
Seeker	Realist (Orphan)	Sleep with one eye open … you never know what is out there.
Lover	Jester	Find a job you enjoy, and you will never have to work a day in your life.
Revolutionary (Destroyer)	Warrior	Anything worth doing is worth doing right, to the best of your ability. (Or: The easiest day you are going to have was yesterday)
Creator	Creator	Necessity is the mother of all invention.
Ruler	Seeker	Boldly go where no man has gone before.
Magician	Idealist (Innocent)	Don't worry, be happy … the sun will come out tomorrow.
Sage	Lover	Group Hug!! (Or: All you need is love!)
Jester	Caregiver	People don't care what you know until they know that you care.

Exercise Seven – The Archetypes and Leadership Style

How would you describe the leadership style of each archetype? What way would they lead? What words would you use to describe their style? Write down your description of their leadership approach. Use the at-a-glance chart to assist you in your work.

Archetype		Your Description of the Archetypes Leadership Style (Clue: What does the archetype value?)
Idealist (Innocent)		
Realist (Orphan)		
Warrior		
Caregiver		
Seeker		
Lover		
Revolutionary (Destroyer)		
Creator		
Ruler		
Magician		
Sage		
Jester		

On the next page, see the author's thoughts on the leadership style of each archetype.

Archetype	The Author's Description of the Archetypes Leadership Style (Clue: What does the archetype value?)
Idealist (Innocent)	Leader Idealist (Innocent) will inspire and desire those they lead to be positive and always looking on the bright side of the day through possibility.
Realist (Orphan)	Leader Realist (Orphan) will inspire and desire those they lead to be vigilant and watchful.
Warrior	Leader Warrior will inspire and desire those they lead to be competitive and battle-sound.
Caregiver	Leader Caregiver will inspire and desire those they lead to be caring and concerned about others.
Seeker	Leader Seeker will inspire and desire those they lead to be inquisitive and adventurous about everything.
Lover	Leader Lover will inspire and desire those they lead to be unified and passionate in their concerns and causes.
Revolutionary (Destroyer)	Leader Revolutionary (Destroyer) will inspire and desire those they lead to be useful and calculating in their work product(s) and process(es).
Creator	Leader Creator will challenge and inspire with creativity those they lead to be as equally creative in their work product(s) or process(es).
Ruler	Leader Ruler will direct and guide with policies and procedures those they lead.
Magician	Leader Magician will inspire those they lead to see what can become of people, projects, or circumstances – they will look to transform someone or something.
Sage	Leader Sage will inspire those they lead to seek truth and the power found in it.
Jester	Leader Jester will inspire those they lead to seek fun and fulfillment in life through the enjoyment of their work and/or projects.

Exercise Eight – The Archetypes and Spilled Coffee

How would each of the archetypes act if they were presented with the same situation? Obviously, we don't want to minimize the complexities of human behavior and all the roots that determine how a person reacts to a set of stimuli. But what would happen if they each had the following situation? Can you predict their behavior in this situation? (The author's thoughts will follow).

Each archetype sees someone walking through the office with a cup of coffee. The person stumbles and spills the coffee down the front of them. How might the archetype respond? What might they say, or what might they do?

Archetype	Your Predicted Response:
Idealist (Innocent)	
Realist (Orphan)	
Warrior	
Caregiver	
Seeker	
Lover	
Revolutionary (Destroyer)	
Creator	
Ruler	
Magician	
Sage	
Jester	

My predicted response of each archetype to the spilled coffee scenario:

Archetype	Author's Predicted response:
Idealist (Innocent)	"It will be okay! Now that Caregiver has cleaned you up, it will still be a great day!!"
Realist (Orphan)	"I have warned you before not to walk too fast. I told someone to fix that carpet!"
Warrior	"I tried to catch you and save the coffee!" (Once they see the coffee has spilled, they may be done with you because you appear unskilled!)
Caregiver	"Are you okay? Is there anything you need? Would you like a new cup of coffee? A new shirt?"
Seeker	"Someone should invent a new way to carry coffee. I've got a great idea on how you can get coffee delivered to you right at your desk."
Lover	"Don't worry about it; I still think you're a great person. I know it might be embarrassing, but I'm still on your side!"
Revolutionary (Destroyer)	"Forget about it and move on. So, you spilled coffee. 'Don't cry over spilled milk,' as they say!"
Creator	"We should invent something that goes over coffee in a cup so you can transport it without spillage! It could be the lid!"
Ruler	"Did you follow the policy? Are you supposed to have coffee in the work area? Did you fill out an accident report?"
Magician	"Can this incident be a defining moment in your life so you can use it to transform the way people view you?"
Sage	"You should note that 22% of all coffee spills in the office are caused by moving too fast in the office!"
Jester	"That was great! Wait until I tell everyone in the break room about this! Do you have another show or was this it?"

Exercise Nine – Archetypes and Accountability

In this exercise, let's predict how an archetype might respond to accountability. How would each archetype respond and handle the world of accountability? This is just a brief look at that interaction, but important for understanding the archetypes and how they might navigate the journey of accountability, which plays a key role in their work on *gap analysis*. This exercise is designed to get the reader to think about a particular archetype and how they might respond to accountability, not necessarily to unlock the mysteries of accountability. Using the at-a-glance chart, how would you complete the following? Regarding accountability, how would each archetype respond in a shadow and strength manner? When would you use the archetype in the strength manner when dealing with accountability? (*Note: Accountability is how someone responds to a set of expectations.*)

Archetype	Shadow	Strength	When to Use
Idealist (Innocent)			
Realist (Orphan)			
Caregiver			
Warrior			
Seeker			
Lover			
Revolutionary (Destroyer)			
Creator			
Ruler			
Magician			
Sage			
Jester			

Here are the author's responses to the way the archetypes would interact with the dynamics of accountability:

Archetype	Shadow	Strength	When to Use
Idealist (Innocent)	Assumes everyone is accountable and might miss the lack of being accountable as they trust everyone to "simply do their jobs."	Will approach others to hold them accountable in a positive and uplifting way to inspire them to meet their obligations.	When others lose hope over expectations and need to be inspired.
Realist (Orphan)	Might only look for places where people will "always" fail in their accountability and become negative, complaining, and overly critical.	They will see the dangers in a lack of accountability and seek to make sure the areas that are lacking are fully covered, and a solution is put in place to prevent it from happening.	When team members don't see the lack of accountability and need someone to speak up about expectations that might not be reached.
Caregiver	Might overly help others who are NOT accountable and make excuses for them. They might simply step in and fulfill the role of those who are not being accountable. They can often enable others to NOT be accountable.	The archetype will genuinely step in to make sure the task, role, and/or items are cared for, and the accountability is covered. They strive to make sure they can help everyone with their requirements and will make sure obstacle(s) are removed.	When others are having trouble meeting expectations and need help accomplish tasks if they can resist enabling them.
Warrior	Might be abusive and taskmasters because they view the lack of accountability as contributing to loss and/or failure to reach a goal. They can be overly direct and demanding.	The archetype is the part inside us that drives us to reach excellence, and accountability is a step toward excellence. They set the example and hold themselves to the highest level of accountability.	When the team is slacking and needs a push over the top. The Warrior can drive others to reach very high expectations.

Seeker	They might leave immediate areas of accountability to seek another vision or mission they dreamed about or saw. They seek to find a new land to conquer and may miss the current responsibilities and process in the search for this new land, idea.	They give us solutions to our responsibilities that we normally would miss. They help us see that responsibility comes in many packages, and there are other avenues to accomplish the task, role, and mission. They look to find new ways to be responsible.	When expectations need to be changed or expanded, and/or enhanced. The Seeker can open the minds of the organization to see new accountabilities and responsibilities.
Lover	They might hold to past methods and fail to meet new expectations and, therefore, look irresponsible. If they don't see the new expectation as allowing them to reach their established values, they might not engage in the needed task, role, and mission.	The Lover supplies us with the passion behind our accountability. They will be very accountable if they see that it will provide a "teaming" atmosphere and allows us all to "express our values" and demonstrate a team atmosphere.	When the demand to meet expectations threatens the organization's harmony.
Revolutionary (Destroyer)	Might simply cut someone loose, or some tasks loose to "cut their losses." The archetype might be quick to disregard an expectation if they believe the procedure and/or approach is no longer useful in their mind.	They will help identify the expectations within the organization that SHOULD be let go and HOW to let them go. They see steps others don't see to dismantle poor or useless expectations.	When an expectation has been identified as needing to be rebuilt or replaced. The Destroyer will supply the framework for the dismantling process.
Creator	This archetype might create a level of expectation that only they see and only they can reach. They tend to own the areas of responsibility they create and dislike any change to their "creation."	When expectations are in demand, the Creator is the one who will develop them. They utilize their skills to further the expectations and to create step-by-step procedures and/or processes.	When there needs to be new expectation(s). The Creator will develop and construct tangible ways to reach the expectations.
Ruler	The Ruler might become ridged and overly structured in their approach to accountability. They tend to find fault with those who miss even the smallest aspects of their policies, procedures, or plans.	They will provide structure and assist in setting a level of expectations. They supply the very fabric of expectations. They have the ability to bring order out of chaos and show others what they are accountable for.	When there is a need for structure and organization of expectations. The Ruler will establish the guidelines and ramifications when expectations are not met.
Magician	They might manipulate those around them to follow expectations even though they don't want to. They might attempt to change those around them to follow "their" expectations for "others."	They have the ability to help others reach a better understanding of their lives and to reach the expectation the individual may "want" to reach. The Magician can help others see the meaning behind the expectation.	When members of the organization do not understand and embrace the reason behind the expectation and need to be transformed to reach them.

Sage	The Sage will not, typically, struggle with expectations unless they believe the expectation is based upon false information or poor thought. If that happens, they will resist the expectation and might believe it is completely foolish.	They will provide the level of knowledge or understanding behind the expectations that allows others to know "why" they are being held accountable. The Sage will give others the truth they need to rise up to accountability.	When there is a lack of intellectual data behind the expectation, the Sage can supply depth when others see the expectation as shallow.
Jester	The archetype might not see the expectation as serious. They might act juvenile or appear insincere about expectations because they see accountability as destructive to their quest for the enjoyment of life.	They add a level of enjoyment to expectations and accountability. They can keep work light and teach others to live light-heartedly in the face of even the most ridged of expectations.	When the desire to hold the team accountable begins to trump the need for enjoyment, refreshment, and/or makes work feel like "work."

Exercise Ten – Archetypes and Conflict

The last exercise is conflict specific. How might each archetype respond to conflict (general conflict)? Again, using the at-a-glance chart, how you would complete this form, like the one on accountability, but focused, instead, on conflict:

Archetype	Shadow	Strength	Advantages in conflict?
Idealist (Innocent)			
Realist (Orphan)			
Caregiver			
Warrior			
Seeker			
Lover			
Revolutionary (Destroyer)			
Creator			
Ruler			
Magician			
Sage			
Jester			

Below are the author's responses.

Archetype	Shadow	Strength	Advantages in conflict?
Idealist (Innocent)	They might miss the conflict and/or stick their head in the sand and refuse to see it.	They see the possibility for resolution in every conflict and the potential if we all just saw the light at the end of the tunnel.	In the midst of difficulty, you offer hope and possibility to those who think only disaster will occur.
Realist (Orphan)	They might only see danger all the time and think if we don't fight this together, we will all lose, so they rally the troops.	They won't be blindsided by the conflict. They will see dangers in a poor solution that might keep us from resolving it.	They bring a sense of realism to the table. They want us to look at things as they are, not "might" be. They keep us safe via practicality.
Caregiver	They might want to concede right away and make sure the other person(s) will have what they need in the conflict; or give them anything to appease the people they serve.	They will be willing to set their pride aside and genuinely care about the other person in the conflict. They try to heal, not hurt. They will want to make sure the values of the organization are helped along.	They offer their caring in a way that calms the anger and slows the aggression. You just can't get mad at a caregiver.
Warrior	They might look for a chance to win and will certainly not want to be the loser in the resolution process.	They will look for the best and most excellent way to resolve the conflict so that everyone believes they will win, and they will fight for that approach.	Using this archetype allows us to put our best foot forward to be seen as a group of people who don't fight each other but fight together for a common cause.
Seeker	They might continually look for alternative solutions in the conflict for resolution. They might spend time brainstorming over and over and over various ways the conflict was caused and solved.	In their search for resolution, they will not be constrained by the status quo, and the *this is the way we always do these things approach*. They want everyone to find adventure in the conflict.	Finding better ways to solve the conflict is, perhaps, the best way to avoid offenses. New ways tend to resist favoring one person's solution over another, thus creating more conflict.
Lover	They might hold onto the conflict too long and too hard. They might focus so long on what caused the conflict that they fail to find a solution to solve it.	The Lover can really embrace others, even at their worst. They will fight for the team and become the glue in many organizations and groups. They won't let a conflict hold back the love/teamwork.	The Lover favors embrace over embattle. Conflicts tend to want to drift apart, but the Lover will use the conflict to draw us together, rallying around a bigger cause.

Archetype	Shadow	Strength	Advantages in conflict?
Revolutionary (Destroyer)	They might stop focusing early on the problem and just want to cut a person loose. They might develop behaviors that are dangerous for them and others and want to cut the cord. They might throw the baby out with the bathwater.	They will be able to get loose from the pain and history of it and know how to just move on. They don't hold grudges and are quick to open a new way to start and to level the old place into a new place to build.	This archetype finds a place to put the pain and to release it so that it no longer hinders us in our growth. They recognize that being angry hurts us more than others, and they teach others "how" to let it go rather than just telling us to "let it go."
Creator	They might focus immediately on the solutions without really understanding the real issues. They will so quickly move to a solution they might miss the hurt the problem caused. Their processes can smother those who hurt.	They can find a real, step-by-step way to solve the problem and put it into practice. They have tangible steps to unpack and repack the issue(s) surrounding the conflict.	Solutions that work when they are practical and tangible. They think that great pain can be released through a visible and tangible method. Creators look for ways to release the conflict and to launch the solution.
Ruler	They might focus on policy and procedure and will miss the people part of the problem. They believe that the issue is solved by sound practices established by law and order. But that law and order can often be controlling and confining.	Will put together sound practices based upon law and order that prevent most conflicts from every happening and will supply concrete guidelines once the solution is established that will prevent the issue from reoccurring.	Good fences make great neighbors. Use this archetype to establish good behavior and good practices that both avoid conflicts and allow you to get back on track and focused on purpose.
Magician	They might see problems and conflicts that aren't problems or conflicts solely for the purpose of healing what ails you. They often over-spiritualize the problem and make a problem a chance for a great show.	They will see the issues behind the problems when others only see the outcomes. They focus on the root, while others are focused on the fruit. They strive to get those in conflict to look within.	Finding the real cause of the conflict will or might make the rules obsolete. When you solve the matters of the heart, it takes care of the issues of the tongue. Fix the attitude and the actions change.
Sage	They might know or believe they know the problems and the solutions simply based on their historical perspective and what they have learned. They might not be ready to recognize new knowledge as that would challenge their established truth.	They want people to know what they are talking about before they start trying to fix something. They become the quality control in the solutions to ensure the solution passes the litmus test they helped to establish.	They truly can find the truth in the conflict and an established and reliable manner to implement that truth. They are very familiar with other patterns or solutions (having studied them) and add energy through their depth of knowledge.
Jester	They might simply want to laugh it off and use their nervous laugh to deflect the real seriousness of the issue. They like to make fun of others amid conflict to avoid facing their own issues.	They add a little levity to keep things easy. They don't take life so seriously and downplay the drama others like to bring. Their desire for enjoyment is contagious and will allow others to heal faster.	Nothing is so serious that it must have drama. Keeping it light and lively allows the serious conflict to heal or, at the minimum, get some needed air. Don't take life so seriously.

Each of the above exercises was designed to increase your ability to not just know the archetypes but to use them within the leadership and follower-ship dynamic. There is no shortcut to learning this material. It is like a new language; the more you use it day-to-day in your practical life, the easier it is navigated. Stretching the language metaphor, the more you use it, the more it is like being able to order a meal at a foreign restaurant and receive a sandwich and not a plunger.

We have one more exercise to do. But that is the one you need to understand the unique correlation between archetypes and *mindset gap analysis*.

PART 2b

12 Archetypes Applied (The connection between mindset and your archetype story)

One of the best take-a-ways from archetype work is how they can unite the story of our lives with our current behavior. I probably overshared more stories in this book than in all three of my earlier books together. The reason for that is twofold: First, I am a compulsive over sharer. Second, I wanted you to see the connection between my life stories, my archetypes and my *beliefs, values, passions, purpose/commitments* and *fears*. Let me remind you about three stories I shared with you, and let's see if you can *figure* me out:

1. I told you the story of my mom coming into my bedroom and telling me that she was divorcing my father so that I would be a preacher or a teacher.
2. I told you the story of my dad taking me to the pump house and telling me I wouldn't be able to do a lot of things in life, but I would be able to outwork anyone.
3. I told you the story of my mom teaching me to care for the poor and my dad insisting on hard work.

With those imprint stories, what archetypes do you think I might use most to navigate my world?

Archetype	David's three brief stories (which archetype and why?)
Idealist (Innocent)	
Realist (Orphan)	
Caregiver	
Warrior	
Seeker	
Lover	
Revolutionary (Destroyer)	
Creator	
Ruler	
Magician	

Sage	
Jester	

If you guessed the *Caregiver-Warrior* pair, you would be very accurate. If you guessed the *Magician* archetype, you would be brilliant! My need to transform my life to fit my mother's *cognitive anchor* was a very large imprint in my life. Hence my current inward desire to transform the lives of others. You see, these life stories do more than leave an imprint on our lives. Our stories shape our archetypes, and our archetypes shape our decisions, and our decisions shape our behaviors.

When we contemplate the stories of our lives, we can connect and realize that it is these stories that give us meaning and understanding about how we frame our journey. Instead of using the *what-pair-of-shoes-do-you-wear* metaphor from the last chapter, let's instead think about each archetype as a car in our garage. Depending on the trip you must take for the day (what event or events are on your calendar), you choose a different car. Our choice of which car, if not always, is decided by how you frame the event and your life story to engage with that event. If you are going to a meeting and need to be more caring or loving, you would take the *Caregiver* or *Lover* archetypes (the minivan). If you decided to take the Hummer, you might have a *mindset* that you are about to go into a meeting where *Warrior* is more suited for the situation. Perhaps this meeting is an innovation meeting, and you need a Jeep to go off-road. You would take the *Seeker* or *Creator* archetypes.

These decisions are all based upon your *mindset* for the situation. Your *mindset*, however, has probably already been set by your *beliefs, values, passions, purpose/commitments* and *fears*. So, we need to ask the question as to the correlation between these archetypes and these *beliefs, values, passions, purpose/commitments* and *fears*.

Let's return to our exercise work from the previous section and have you complete one more worksheet. This worksheet is another main take-away of this book. Please take a good amount of time to complete this form. Use the at-a-glance worksheet from the earlier section (pages 32-34). I will eventually give you *some suggested* answers. But they are only *my* thoughts. Yours might be different and still be healthy and profitable for your work situation. Remember, you are using your collective *thought river* to make your decisions on these questions. You can see these through your *archetypal* lens, as well.

One way to do the work on this sheet is to start with the archetype's *fear* first. It is easier if you start with your perceptions of what they might *fear* and then work your way back. Remember, we *fear* whatever we think will not allow us to reach our *purpose/commitment*.

It is also easier if you work through an archetype that has more meaning to you. If you took the Pearson-Marr Archetype Inventory (PMAI)®, you can start with the archetypes at the top of your report. If you didn't take the inventory, please start with the one or two archetypes that resonate with you. Once you complete a row for one or two of the archetypes, continue to read. I am going to use the Magician archetype as an example after you work on your op archetypes. So, try to think through that archetype, as well.

Archetype Mindset Worksheet					
Identify:	**Their belief** (What do they hold to be true at the root of my life?)	**Their value** (What do they give the greatest priority, emphasis in life?)	**Their passion** (What is driving the internal emotion that gives them energy?)	**Their purpose or commitment** (What is the obligatory action they must take daily?)	**Their Fear** (What do they fear that might prevent their commitment?)
Idealist **(Innocent)**					
Realist **(Orphan)**					
Caregiver					
Warrior					
Seeker					
Lover					
Revolutionary **(Destroyer)**					
Creator					

Ruler					
Magician					
Sage					
Jester					

As an example, let's work through the Magician archetype and see how you did. Reflecting on the at-a-glance sheets (pages 32-34), we discover that the key words for the *Magician* are *transformer, catalyst for change, healer*. So, if the *Magician* wants to go around *healing* and *changing* things, what do they *fear*? If they really want to *transform* someone or something, what or WHO might they *fear*? Remember, we fear anyone or anything that prevents us from reaching our *purpose/commitment* in life. If I am using the tool of the *Magician* to navigate my day, then I am *committed* to *transforming* and *healing* and *changing* things. So, what/who do I *fear*? I *fear* anyone or any group of people who do not want to *transform*, *heal* or *change*. Regarding my *mindset gap* this is very informative. Regarding my *bridging* my *mindset gaps* this is vital.

For the first 20 years of doing this type of work, I would say I was able to connect and work with everyone I came across as a client; except four people. You may think that is an extremely low number for 20 years of work. You might also think, however, that it is a very exact number. Why did I know there were *four*? And more importantly, why didn't I connect and work with them? It was not until I understood this *mindset gap analysis* work that I realized it was not them; it was me. (Most of you reading this book probably arrived at that conclusion much earlier than I did, by just reading a few pages). You see, if I perceive that someone I am trying to connect with and work with (for the purpose of transformation) is only going through the motions and does not really want to change, I simply walked away from them. (How sad!) It was not until I knew that about myself (what I *fear* and my *mindset gap analysis*) that I was able to close that *gap* (more on that later).

Identify:	Their belief (What do they hold to be true at the root of my life?)	Their value (What do they give the greatest priority, emphasis in life?)	Their passion (What is driving the internal emotion that gives them energy?)	Their purpose or commitment (What is the obligatory action they must take daily?)	Their Fear (What do they fear that might prevent their commitment?)
Magician					**People and/or organizations that don't want to change.**

61

Now let's move to the first column and decide what *a* core belief might be for the *Magician*. (Note: Everyone has more than one belief, and that is certainly true of all archetypal imprints. But, for the sake of this work, we are simply trying to create a general formula we can use to identify *mindset gaps*.) If the *Magician fears* people and/or organizations that don't want to change, what could they possibly believe at the core of their life? In truth, to transform and/or change something or someone, you must first believe that someone or something *needs* to be changed. So, the *Magician* has a core *belief* as:

Identify:	Their belief (What do they hold to be true at the root of my life?)	Their value (What do they give the greatest priority, emphasis in life?)	Their passion (What is driving the internal emotion that gives them energy?)	Their purpose or commitment (What is the obligatory action they must take daily?)	Their Fear (What do they fear that might prevent their commitment?)
Magician	Everything can be better than it is currently.				People and/or organizations that don't want to change

Stop for a moment and think about this core *belief* of the *Magician*. If you had a team member on your staff who identified with the *Magician* archetype, what type of work might excite them? What type of work might suck the life out of them? Suppose you told them their daily task was to *change* the office by painting it, purchasing new furniture, or any other modifications for the sole purpose that will *transform* the very ethos of the office culture. Or suppose you told them to just sit and watch the paint dry and maintain the status quo. If you want to get the energy level of the *Magician* higher, give them a role that is *transforming*. That will resonate with this core *belief*.

However, at the root of their life, Magicians believe everything can be better. Can you think of a downside to that *belief*? Suppose a *Magician* came home from work one day and said to their spouse: "*Honey, I think you can be better*!" That would not go over well. (More on that later, as well.) That is the downside of this core *Magician's belief* system. If you walk around and think everything can be better than it is currently, you may eventually start to believe that no one, or anything, is good enough. Do you see this *mindset gap* for the *Magician*? You might say to your team member *Magician*, "*That's all good; we are done with this process, product or procedure. Let's move to the next stage or phase.*"

The *Magician* may not move on as eagerly as the rest of the team does. Verbally you are holding a sign that reads, "*Let's move on now.*" But the *Magician* may be holding their own sign that reads like this:

You see, our *beliefs* all sound great, but they can have a shadowy side. We will see this more in the following pages as we dive deeper into the beliefs of the other archetypes.

Before we move on to the next columns for the *Magician*, let me repeat something I mentioned earlier in the book. I openly admit I am drawing a very distinct difference in nuances of the definition between a *belief*, a *value*, a *passion*, a *purpose* and/or *commitment*, and a *fear*. We far too often just roll these terms into the same pathways of our *mindset*. That is probably not that unhealthy. When we talk to someone, we seldom detect the *nuances* of their language. We might do that in our legal documents, but not in normal, healthy conversations. However, when we are attempting to *bridge* a *mindset gap*, I would maintain success is more than not in the *nuances*. Too many people write development plans for employees (IDPs) who are obviously in a *gap* situation yet pay little attention to the words we use in each improvement phase. Let me give you one example of this that was recently discovered in work with a client.

This client had the role of supervising and monitoring work done by teachers in her county. In fact, her job title was a *supervisor* (she was on a *supervisor* pay scale). Her job description said she was to *monitor* compliance in the county. But her immediate supervisor wanted her to be more of a *coach* to those she was *monitoring*. Since this individual was much more comfortable living in the *Sage* and *Ruler* world, she was very equipped *archetypally* to fulfill the *monitor* role. However, what her organization wanted was *coaching* those in the county to get them to reach compliance. She approached the role as a *Sage-Ruler* (after all, she thought, "My job titled is *supervisor!*"). She thought her role was to hold people accountable (she was THE *monitor* in the county). But the *mindset gap* was discovered when I was told that the organization really wanted her to *coach* teachers in the county (that is more the *Magician* archetype). *Nuance* matters! This staff member didn't have a challenge doing what she thought the job was when she was hired. Using language to understand the *gap analysis* better equipped her to perform the required role in the best way. She did have to monitor those in the county, but she really needed to coach those in the county. That is less *Ruler* and more *Magician*.

With this concept of *nuance matters* in our minds, let's return to the *Magician*. If the *Magician believes* all things can be better than they are at the current moment and they *fear* anyone who will not transform or change, what do they *value?* For this work, I am simply looking for one word that would convey an archetype's particular *value*. All archetypes *value* more than a one-word *value*, of course. But, at this point, we are only trying to think through a pattern of thought for an archetype.

Magicians value *change*. In fact, that is their greatest strength, as well as their Achilles heel. They so much want change for people and organizations they can often fail to realize they are trying to change things others don't really want to change (i.e., "*Honey, I think you can be better!*") They are constantly *believing* that things can be better, and they push for change in some of the most unusual and untimely ways.

Identify:	Their belief (What do they hold to be true at the root of my life?)	Their value (What do they give the greatest priority, emphasis in life?)	Their passion (What is driving the internal emotion that gives them energy?)	Their purpose or commitment (What is the obligatory action they must take daily?)	Their Fear (What do they fear that might prevent their commitment?)
Magician	Everything can be better than it is currently.	**Change**			People and/or organizations that don't want to change.

Remember, the *Magician* has some story at their core that drives this *belief* and *value*. Other archetype imprints don't think like this. C*hange*, to the *Magician*, flows from the core of their *belief* structure. This is why they *value* anything having to do with *change*. Now you may understand why my *Magician* journey caused me to write my second book on the topic of *change* (*Archetypes and the Drama of Change*; The Book Publishing Pros).

So, what is the *Magician's passion*? How will it come out in a visible and tangible *purpose/commitment*? This is the *Magician's mindset* composition:

Identify:	Their belief (What do they hold to be true at the root of my life?)	Their value (What do they give the greatest priority, emphasis in life?)	Their passion (What is driving the internal emotion that gives them energy?)	Their purpose or commitment (What is the obligatory action they must take daily?)	Their Fear (What do they fear that might prevent their commitment?)
Magician	Everything can be better than it is currently	Change	**Transforming people and organizations.**	**Moving people & organizations from point A to point B.**	People and/or organizations that don't want to change

As we look at how the *Magician is built*, we can see the small *nuances* between the *belief, value, passion, purpose/commitment* and *fears*. This is not all of what makes the *Magician* who they are, but this is a core aspect of their *mindset* that flows from their *thought river*. That *thought river* is full of stories that allow us to understand how their mind might be constructed regarding *activities* we are asking them to do. It might tell us why they have a *fixed* or *fluid mindset*. More importantly, this helps us find potential *mindset gaps* they have. If you hire, retain, promote or work with in any capacity with someone driving the *Magician* car, coming to every meeting wearing the *Magician* shoes, and/or using the *Magician* tools to navigate their world, you can be assured they will be energized by work that *transforms* the world around them (no matter how big or small that world). And you will create a *gap* if they can't find a way to use their *belief* and *value* in some way. Here are some examples of a *Magician* transforming the world around them:

Life coach – *using principles to transform*

Landscape artist – *using bark, fountains, flowers, etc., to transform*

Beautician – *using color, curls, hot irons, etc., to transform*

House flipping – *using timber, paint, plumbing, etc., to transform*

Youth Sports coach – *using balls, whistles and games to transform*

Religious leaders – *using dogma to transform*

There are hundreds of occupations, hobbies and interests where the *Magician* can fulfill their *belief, value, passion, purpose/commitment*. But no matter the occupation, hobby and/or interest the *Magician* has in their aim, their result...*change*. And, without a doubt, they will *fear* anything or anyone that tries to prevent them from carrying out that *transformation*.

Let's do another exercise. Not only does the *Magician* have a particular pathology, but so do the other archetypes. Use the following chart to do some analysis on each of the archetypes we are using in this work to help identify *mindset gaps*:

Archetypes and Mindset Analysis

Identify:	Their belief (What do they hold to be true at the root of my life?)	Their value (What do they give the greatest priority, emphasis in life?)	Their passion (What is driving the internal emotion that gives them energy?)	Their commitment (What is the obligatory action they must take daily?)	Their Fear (What do they fear that might prevent their commitment?)
Idealist (Innocent)					
Realist (Orphan)					
Caregiver					
Warrior					
Seeker					
Lover					
Revolutionary (Destroyer)					
Creator					
Ruler					
Magician					
Sage					
Jester					

It is important to realize that there is more than one belief, one value, etc., for each archetype. As you go through the above exercise, it is not important that you match what I have written in my responses below. This will be especially true if you are working through the above chart with a particular direct-report and/or team member in mind. You might want to think of yourself first, however. How does this fit into your life journey? If you took the PMAI®, as mentioned earlier, you might want to start with your top archetype (or top three) and think through each of the columns. If you have not taken the inventory, pick the archetype that best resonates with your life path and fill in the box. Ask yourself these questions to walk through your own reflective work. Remember, it is easier if you start with what you might know about an *archetype* and consider the *fear* first. (You can simply go to my *answer key,* but I think that would deprive you of some good *mindset* processing work.) When you consider the archetype of _____:

> **Question**: What is something you think may *shut that archetype down*? When this archetype is at its best, what might they *fear* that causes them to simply stop and be less and less energized? This is something they perceive that would take them off their designed course for life. Their *fear*!

> **Question**: What is at the core of what makes this archetype who they are? What is their very core *belief*? This would be something that they have learned is a *belief* that gives them true meaning in life.

> **Question**: What is one word this archetype might pick to define their priority for life? What is their primary *value*? When you think about this, put this archetype on, like a pair of shoes. If you were using this archetype to navigate your daily path, what would be a driving *value* that would drive your daily choices?

> **Question**: What would this archetype be doing when they are the most energized in life? What is their *passion?* What really excites them? What will fuel their inner being? If you saw them doing something so very naturally, what would that thing be?

> **Question**: What does this archetype want to do, most of their day? What is their *purpose* and/or *commitment*? These are the actionable behaviors you might see in their life each day. This is what they might do, not as their job description or assignment for the day, but what they end up pivoting toward each day. This is the thing that might answer this question for them, at the end of the day: Today I received my most energy from _____!

My responses and thoughts about each archetype are on the next page:

Archetype Mindset Worksheet					
Identify:	**Their belief** (What do they hold to be true at the root of my life?)	**Their value** (What do they give the greatest priority, emphasis in life?)	**Their passion** (What is driving the internal emotion that gives them energy?)	**Their commitment** (What is the obligatory action they must take daily?)	**Their Fear** (What do they fear that might prevent their commitment?)
Idealist (Innocent)	Anything is possible	Hope	Finding possibility in the midst of all circumstances	Making sure their positivity spills over to others	Lack of hope and/or negative people
Realist (Orphan)	A dangerous life can be overcome by watchfulness	Vigilance	Keeping the world around them safe	Spotting danger before anyone else	Ignoring danger
Caregiver	Everyone needs help	Selflessness	Helping others succeed in their needs/dreams	Being available to anyone, anytime	Being told they can't help
Warrior	Performance matters	Excellence	Achieving the best	Meeting any challenge	Laziness and/or mediocrity
Seeker	There is something to be discovered	Journey	Discovery	Finding something new/different	Status quo
Lover	We are created to connect to others	Relationships	Holding on to something they value	Holding on to people/things with deep relationships	Anything that might damage relationships
Revolutionary (Destroyer)	When something is failing, improve it	Efficiency	Improvement	Recognizing and correcting the no longer profitable	Doing something that is unprofitable and/or useless
Creator	There is something tangible that is yet to be created	Practical Imagination	Taking an idea and bringing it to fruition	Using all available resources to create something	Lack of resources or support for their creations
Ruler	Life should have order	Structure	Organizing people and things	Turning disorder into order	People and/or organizations that tolerate chaos
Magician	Everything can be better than it is currently	Change	Transforming people and organizations	Moving people & organizations from point A to point B	People and/or organizations that don't want to change
Sage	Knowledge is power	Learning	Thirst for knowing	Offering their knowledge to cause intellectual growth	Lack of a desire to learn and/or incompetent people
Jester	Life should be enjoyed	Enjoyment	Embracing a zeal and zest for life	Making life enjoyable for the world around them	Taking life and/or work too seriously

The above responses are not offered as authoritative in any way. I would simply say that in my past 30 years of coaching others, I have come to these general themes. These themes give us a general framework to not only better understand an archetypal imprint but also how to use the knowledge about our *mindset gap* analysis work. To do that work, we have to take the knowledge we learn from the *mindset* diagram, the general *archetype* understanding, and the work regarding an archetype's *beliefs, values, passions, purpose/commitments* and/or *fears*.

Before we move into Part 4 and put all this together, let me add one more thought about the above material. To show just how important it is to identify the *beliefs, values, passions, purpose/commitments* and/or *fears* of a co-worker, teammate, direct report, etc., let me return to our brief stories of *Bill, Julie* and *Ken*, from the Preface. Let's go back and remember their brief story again. But, this time, I will give you a little more information. Let's see if you can identify their *beliefs, values, passions, purpose/commitments* and/or *fear*. Here is a synopsis:

Bill
Remember his story? He is fearful that he will do something wrong. His life journey had brought him to a place where he was fearful that he might have done something improper and his superintendent would be taking him to task for it. What I didn't tell you the first time is that he called me to tell me that he remembered a story of when he was in 1st grade. He was supposed to read along in that old reading book series, "Read with Dick and Jane." The teacher would have him read aloud with three other boys. As the teacher ran her pencil over the words, Bill, in unison with the other boys, was supposed to read the Dick and Jane words out loud. However, Bill missed kindergarten and was far behind. When the teacher noticed that Bill was just trying to mimic the other three boys and not really reading the words, she would thump him in the forehead with the eraser end of the pencil. Regarding Bill's fear of doing anything wrong, he said to me, emotionally, "I think I simply don't want to get thumped in the head for making a mistake."

The archetype you think impacts their story:	What is their *belief*? What do they hold to be true at the root of their life?	What is their *value*? What do they give the greatest priority, emphasis in life?	What is their *passion*? What is driving the internal emotion that gives them energy?	What is their *purpose* and/or *commitment*? What is the obligatory action they must take daily?	What is their *fear*? What do they fear that might prevent their commitment?

	Julie

Remember her story? She has a great desire and is bent on helping others. But it is not just to help them. She is fearful that the work won't get done and the organization won't reach its goals. She tends to step in to make sure that others have the help they need to get the work done in a way that the work is done and done right. What I didn't tell you concerns her childhood and the impact her father and stepmom had on her current behavior. When she was a child, she was singled out (as the lone stepchild in the home) for her work performance. If she did the dishes and her parental authority found one spot on a dish on a finished dish Julie had put into the cupboard, they would make her do the dish again to make sure there were NO spots. But not just that dish. All the dishes she also completed. The same was true about weeding the garden. If she missed a weed, they would make her go back to the beginning and walk the entire garden again to make there were NO weeds.

The archetype you think impacts their story:	What is their *belief*? What do they hold to be true at the root of their life?	What is their *value*? What do they give the greatest priority, emphasis in life?	What is their *passion*? What is driving the internal emotion that gives them energy?	What is their *purpose* and/or *commitment*? What is the obligatory action they must take daily?	What is their *fear*? What do they fear that might prevent their commitment?

Ken					
Remember his story? Ken was/is a top-notch HR manager in a growing organization, but he had a passion that was being restricted by the *thought river* of his *mindset*. He wanted to be creative and use his creativity. In fact, in his earlier years, he dreamed of authoring a book or developing something from his creative mind. However, through this *mindset gap analysis* work, Ken realized this creative desire was shut down, and it centered around his former supervisor, the previous owner of the company. Under the previous owner, when he offered to do something in the creative world, she would say to him, "*That is not your strong skill set. I need you to focus on HR things and let me do the creative work.*" As we worked through *gap analysis* (and especially Part 3), Ken realized that he not only had a passion to do some creative work, but he decided to write a book. He would focus on the best HR practices he had developed over the years. His plan was to present it to the new owner of the company and use it as a marketing tool for new clients (most of this organization's clients did not have their own HR director and could use this material).					

The archetype you think impacts their story:	**What is their *belief*?** What do they hold to be true at the root of their life?	**What is their *value*?** What do they give the greatest priority, emphasis in life?	**What is their *passion*?** What is driving the internal emotion that gives them energy?	**What is their *purpose* and/or *commitment*?** What is the obligatory action they must take daily?	**What is their *fear*?** What do they fear that might prevent their commitment?

How did you work through Bill, Julie and Ken's stories? Did you find their *belief, value, passion, purpose/commitment* and/or *fear*? Did you spot their primary archetype? We will visit these three one more time at the end of the next section. At the end of Part 3, we will walk through each of their stories again, in detail, as we unfold a step-by-step matrix for change. The following section marries Part 1, Part 2a and Part 2b into a systematic way to build a bridge for *mindset gaps*.

PART 3
Renewing the Mind

How you are primed determines the direction we are aimed.

(Another of David's life laws)

At this point, if I could, I would take you to our boat in Florida. We slip our second home (a boat) on the Gulf side, and we love to go into the Gulf to search for dolphins. In a recent trip with my granddaughter, Harlow, we took the boat out and found a pod of dolphins. She thought it was so cool that I, her *Bumpa,* could find these amazing animals and even get them to follow the boat and jump in our wake. (The one in the picture followed us for about two miles.) The truth of the matter (and please don't tell Harlow) is that dolphins have been jumping the wakes of boats for centuries. They just must jump wakes. It is what they do. It is how they are *primed.*

Being *primed* can be understood that we have been stimulated to do or think something based upon another set of stimuli. We typically and subconsciously respond in a predictable manner. So, if I show you the below image, you will probably know the missing color.

The missing color is _____?

How did I know you were going to pick yellow?

Being *primed* in our *mindset* is the content of this book. Our *ever-changing and moving historical river of past experiences and accumulated knowledge* (our *thought river*) has *primed* us to respond in certain ways, at certain times, and in a most redundant fashion. With all the talk we have about our free will, we still can't seem to stop eating that one food group at night before bed, doing that one thing we do that irritates our spouse, or that one area our employer spoke to us about in our last evaluation.

The educational world relies on the healthier side of *priming*. A Hebrew Rabbi would use an aspect of *priming* to teach their dogma. They called it a *Remez*. The word *Remez* means *hint*. When a Rabbi teaches their typical audience, they would know that those present were so familiar with what they were teaching that they only had to refer to a portion of their written doctrines, and their audience would be able to recall the material. Because the audience was *primed* for the entire portion of their teaching, the Rabbi only had to say a part, and the audience was right with them. They only had to give them a *hint*. They were *primed* to know the material, only hearing a part of it.

Let's illustrate a *Remez* this way, using nursery rhymes:

Humpty Dumpty sat on the…

Jack and Jill went up the…

There was an old woman who lived in a…

Twinkle, Twinkle Little…

Row, row, row your…

You don't need to hear the rest of the rhyme to know what it is about. The first part that I shared with you is a Remez. It relies on you being primed for the rest of the nursery song. But, if you have never heard the song or the rhyme, you would not have any idea what was to follow. This is the good and the bad of a Remez, the hint. A Remez relies on how you were primed. Education relies on the power of the Remez, the hint. In testing, a teacher refers to something on the test (a Remez), and the student answers the question correctly (or so they hope).

If my above-life law is accurate (The way we are primed determines the direction we are aimed), this priming can be healthy or unhealthy. When we need prime behaviors to be consistent and to follow the hints we get for life's situations, it can be a very good thing. However, if we have developed a prime that does not fit our new role in an organization, our new job description, or our new leadership requirements, prime can be unhealthy. Prime can be harder to change than any habit we want to break (think about the illustration from the last section, the Sage-Ruler-supervisor-monitor who needed to become a coach instead of a supervisor). Sometimes life requires us to change this prime...this mindset that has formed around archetypal imprints. We must find a way, at times, to renew our minds.

When it comes to our *mindset gap analysis* work, this *renewing* of our *prime* is a key for us to determine the cause of a *mindset gap*. Even more importantly, it is essential to know the *prime* so we know how to *bridge* the *gap*. To facilitate this, let me introduce you to a systematic way we could use to ease the *renewing of our mindsets*. There are two areas of concern to the work: The first is to identify the old patterns of thoughts (i.e., *cognitive anchors, assumed constraints,* and/or our *oychroma,* based upon the *archetype* imprints that determined our *beliefs, values, passions, purpose/commitments* and *fears.*). We must genuinely dive deeper into why we think the way we think. The second is to rebuild these *beliefs, values, passions, purpose/commitments* and *fears,* for the purpose of constructing new *mindsets* that better fit our situation for life at work, home or play. We do this second part by pouring new *archetypal* stories into our *thought river*.

Doing both these steps is not rocket science, but it does call for some hard work of introspection and rebuilding. Remember a thought that was mentioned earlier in the book: Most *of the time, to go higher, you must go deeper*. Most people just want to go higher. They seldom want to go deeper.

To help your learning of this system (a matrix), I am going to apply each phase of this matrix to four more clients *as well as* myself (I can't expect you to go deeper if I won't). Upon conclusion with these four, we will apply each phase to our earlier clients, also (Bill, Julie and Ken).

Here are four wonderful clients (plus me) who will walk you through their experience with each phase of the matrix. I hope you can glean from their deeper, introspective work insights for your own journey:

Jeff – A high school principal in a k-12 school that was brought on to replace a retiring curmudgeon. The superintendent hiring Jeff really wanted an idea guy. He nailed it by hiring Jeff. However, two years later, a new superintendent arrived and wanted my help to *fix* Jeff's failure to listen to anyone else's ideas. It appeared that Jeff's *ochyroma* was to come up with ideas. But why?

Amy – An elementary principal who was, a few months before I met her, in a central office position as a curriculum director at a k-12 school. Amy hired me herself. In her mind, this principalship was a demotion. In her superintendent's mind, this was the last stop before her contract ran out. She asked me to help her say, "No!" Apparently, as the curriculum director, she gave in to every request. During the start of the elementary principal role, she was doing the same thing. She needed help, fast! It appeared that Amy's *ochyroma* was to say yes to everyone. But why?

Mitch – An ex-NFL football player who had to lose weight. He met with me at a sports bar for lunch and had just ordered a burger, fries and a beer. He had been out of the NFL for a few years and had *blossomed* a bit. The doctor was worried about his back, his knees and his overall health. He was told he had to lose about 50 lbs. probably more, but let's go with that. He didn't want to go on a diet to lose weight. It appeared that Mitch's *ochyroma* was to eat. But why?

Erik – A son of one of my clients, Erik, worked in a tool and die company. He attended a career tech high school and was quite a quick learner. He was hired by this company right out of high school. He was promoted two or three times and, when I met him, was leading a small team of five other staff. His father recognized that he had never had any leadership experience. He wanted me to expand his leadership capacity. But his father was worried that his son would leave the company and want to start his own business. The irony is that Erik was not a risk taker, and he wanted me to help him become a risk taker. It appeared that Erik's *ochyroma* was making sure he was comfortable. But why?

David – Me! I was told by my ex-wife to stop trying to fix everyone (enter the activity and mission of the *Magician* into our marriage at about the seven-year mark). Of course, the person I *apparently* was trying to fix was her. (Please don't hate me.) She thought I should stop trying to fix her and everyone else I met. It appears that David's *ochyroma* was to transform (fix) everyone. But why?

These will be our four (five counting me) *test cases* for this section as we walk through this seven-phase matrix system. It should be noted that each of these four individuals had already done some good work centered around their *thought river* and how their *mindset* was built. As they worked through the following system, they had to face their current *mindset*, their *cognitive anchors,* and *assumed constraints*. They had to investigate their *oychroma* and their more active *archetype imprints*. We had *primed* them to look deeper into their *mindset* with the material covered in Parts 1 and 2.

I will state boldly that this next part is not to be a *read-only* section. This is real work to be done and completed to learn this process. I invite you to take out a pen and use the worksheets I am providing. Or better, open a document to create your own worksheet, like what you are about to read.

The Individual Transformation Matrix – Phase 1

(Notice how I used the word transformation… can you say, Magician?)

To start the renewal of the mindset process, let's ask one simple question:

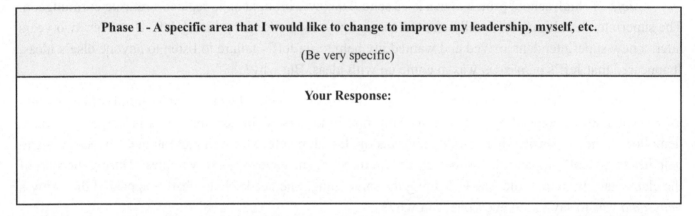

Phase 1 - A specific area that I would like to change to improve my leadership, myself, etc.
(Be very specific)
Your Response:

This needs to be, as said, very specific. Don't be general or vague, or ambiguous. This will be important as we work through the challenge. It will be important as we unfold each phase. At times, people like to stay vague because it tends to allow them to finish *in the ballpark*. But in this work, we want to make some intentional changes that are identifiable and/or measurable at the end. If you want to create your own spreadsheet or table to work through this material, that might help as you think through the process. For your personal work, this will be two separate boxes, as shown above. However, for our five test cases, it will look like this. Each of the test cases has one area that they want to improve:

Phase 1 - A specific area that I would like to change to improve my leadership, myself, etc.				
(Be very specific)				
Jeff	**Amy**	**Mitch**	**Erik**	**David**
I need to listen to the ideas of others.	Being a stronger leader by saying *no* sometimes.	I need to lose 50 lbs.	Become a leader who is a *risk taker*.	Quit trying to fix people.

As you can see, they each have a defined challenge to address. Jeff was told, by his superintendent, that he had to listen to the ideas of others. This was not his choice. He was not a very willing participant in the transformation process. (How do you think that started with him not wanting to transform and me, being the *Magician*, who lives to transform?)

Amy really wanted to keep her job, so she was highly motivated to transform.

Mitch was told by a doctor to lose weight. I had my doubts that he was that enthusiastic.

Erik was highly motivated but really didn't want to define what he meant by taking a *risk*.

When my ex-wife told me to stop fixing others, I was not motivated at all. By the time I discovered this *gap* that needed to be addressed, she had already filed for a divorce. However, after being remarried, to an amazing woman, I was highly motivated to dig deeper into what had happened the last time. I did not want a repeat performance this time around.

Phase 2 of the transformation matrix is as follows:

Phase 1 - A specific area that I would like to change to improve my leadership, myself, etc.			
(Be very specific)			
Your Response:			
Phase 2 – What do I need to do more of, less of, stop doing, or start doing to make #1 happen?			
What should I do more of?	What should I do less of?	What should I stop doing?	What should I start doing?

Jeff, Amy, Mitch and Erik will need to produce a more of, less of, stop doing and start doing action (M-L-S-S) to complete their work. As will you for your work. But, for our example (and time and space), we are simply going to use *one* of those four to illustrate their journey into the deeper end of their *mindset*. You should complete the above table by coming up with something for each M-L-S-S. Our examples look like this:

	Phase 1 - A specific area that I would like to change to improve my leadership, myself, etc. (Be very specific)				
	Jeff	**Amy**	**Mitch**	**Erik**	**David**
	I need to listen to the ideas of others.	Being a stronger leader by saying *no* sometimes.	I need to lose 50 lbs.	Become a leader who is a *risk taker*.	Quit trying to fix people.
	Phase 2 – What do I need to do to impact Phase 1?				
	More of:	**Less of:**	**Stop doing:**	**Start doing:**	**Stop doing?**
By doing these things I can better accomplish my Phase 1 challenge					

Before I simply give you their answers, take some time to insert what **you think** they should do M-L-S-S. (Remember, they each had to answer all four, but we are using one of their four for our example. Using myself as another example, I simply selected to supply only one, as well: A *stop doing*.)

What do you think they answered? Jeff had a really challenging time with this. When you read his response, you will see how flimsy it appears. Amy's is obvious, as was Mitch and Erik's. Mine is less obvious but highly accurate. The key in Phase 2 is that whatever you commit to in the M-L-S-S exercise, it MUST affect the challenge in Phase 1. You should be able to say, "Yes, if I this happened, it would definitely impact Phase 1!"

Don't forget to work on your own process, as well. What is it that will impact your Phase 1? What is it that you know you could do *more of,* and it would change Phase 1? What is it that you are currently doing too much of, and you should do *less of* that would affect Phase 1? What do you do that you should simply *stop doing* that could really alter Phase 1? And what is something you could *start doing* that would be a game changer and transform your Phase 1?

Here is what each of our test case studies stated.

Phase 1 - A specific area that I would like to change to improve my leadership, myself, etc.					
				(Be very specific)	
	Jeff	**Amy**	**Mitch**	**Erik**	**David**
	I need to listen to the ideas of others.	Being a stronger leader by saying *no* sometimes.	I need to lose 50 lbs.	Become a leader who is a *risk taker*.	Quit trying to fix people.
	Phase 2 – What do I need to do to impact Phase 1?				
	More of:	**Less of:**	**Stop doing:**	**Start doing:**	**Stop doing?**
By doing these things I can better accomplish my Phase 1 challenge	Give those who come in and talk with me, or meet me in the hallway, my undivided and full attention.	Worrying about what others think about me.	Eating at fast food restaurants.	Something I have never done before.	Looking at others as though they have a problem.

As you can see, each of them had something that would impact Phase 1. Jeff was still not all in on this work, but he did agree that if he did give people good attention, it would *appear* that he was listening to their ideas. (I had my doubts.) In the case of Amy, that really was her big challenge. She was so worried about how her staff felt about her she just always said *yes* to anything and everything. Mitch (remember we were at a sports bar, and he had ordered a burger, fries and a beer) was serious. But I didn't think his *stop-doing* was really going to make the impact he wanted. Like most who try losing weight, eating less is always a good *go-to*. Erik's made perfect sense, but he had no idea what *doing something he had never done before* looked like. As for me, well, you can see the issue, correct?

Here is an interesting aspect of the M-L-S-S exercise: It is a small confessional booth. By listing these things and writing them out, each of our individuals is telling us what they are not doing enough, what they are doing too much of, what they should not be doing (but are), and what they should be doing (but are not). Each of the areas are what you might read in a *self-help* book. Each chapter of said *self-help* book would have a chapter heading that said to do more of this and to do less of that, and stop doing this and start doing that. The struggle centers on the fact that IF anyone could do *more of, less of, stop doing* and *start doing*, they probably would. Typically, our *prime* is not allowing us to *aim* in the direction of these *more of, less of, stop doing* and *start doing* lists.

So, whatever you recorded as your M-L-S-S, it was a confession that these are things with which you are already struggling. That is not a bad thing. It is a healthy activity to identify these areas. This is especially true if you want to change the challenge you outlined in Phase 1 of this matrix. The point of the matter is that we are not doing these things, and we know we should be. But *why* are we not doing these things?

Remember our discussion about our *purpose/commitment* and our relationship with *fear*? We mentioned Dr. Robert Kegan's work on *Immunity to Change*. The premise was that we *fear* anything that prevents us from reaching or accomplishing our *commitment*. So, what if the areas we outlined in Phase 2 as our M-L-S-S work were contrary to our subconscious *mindset* and ran contrary to our *purpose/commitment*? Someone could tell us all day to do **more of** this, and we would not because we *fear* it will prevent us from reaching our *purpose/commitment*. Someone could tell us all day to do **less of** this, and we would not because we *fear* it will prevent us from reaching our *purpose/commitment*. Someone could tell us all day to **stop doing** this, and we would not because we *fear* it will prevent us from reaching our *purpose/commitment*. Someone could tell us all day to **start doing** that, and we would not because we *fear* it will prevent us from reaching our *purpose/commitment*. This is exactly what is challenging about many of the individual development plans (IDP) we put together to improve our team members' performance. We don't realize we are simply asking them to do M-L-S-S exercises. It is often not that they don't want to do the lists of items on an IDP; it is that for most of the M-L-S-S on the IDP, we ask them to create cuts across the *purpose/commitment* that flows from their *thought river*. Often, they have already been *primed* to NOT do those things. Plus, typically, if they could do those things, they would, and you would not need the IDP!

That means we must overcome the *fear* that is preventing us from accomplishing our M-L-S-S list. So, the next step in our work is to identify that *fear*.

Here is the next step in our work sheet:

Phase 1 - A specific area that I would like to change to improve my leadership, myself, etc. (Be very specific)					
	Jeff	**Amy**	**Mitch**	**Erik**	**David**
	I need to listen to the ideas of others.	Being a stronger leader by saying *no* sometimes.	I need to lose 50 lbs.	Become a leader who is a *risk taker*.	Quit trying to fix people.
	Phase 2 – What do I need to do to impact Phase 1?				
	More of:	**Less of:**	**Stop doing:**	**Start doing:**	**Stop doing?**
By doing these things I can better accomplish my Phase 1 challenge	Give those who come in and talk with me or meet me in the hallway my undivided and full attention.	Worrying about what others think about me.	Eating at fast food restaurants.	Something I have never done before.	Looking at others as though they have a problem.
My big **FEAR** that prevents me from doing the above is:					

Why do you think Jeff would *fear* doing more listening and giving others focused attention? Why do you think Amy would *fear* dosing less worrying about what others think of her? Why do you think Mitch would *fear* to stop eating at fast food restaurants? Why do you think Erik would *fear* to start doing something he had never done before? Why do you think I would *fear* to stop looking at others as though they had a problem? You will probably spot what they should write in their box rather easily. In fact, when we use this system to help others grow, it is easy to spot another person's *fear*. It was not so easy for Jeff, Amy, Mitch, or Erik to identify their own *fear*. I struggled also. (But now I understand it incredibly well since I understand my archetype imprints much better than I did during this deep, dark chapter of my life.)

How are you doing at identifying your own *fears?* Remember, each of these case studies needed to do all four of the M-L-S-S portions of their chart. You should have, as well. So, you have four *fears* to identify. How are you doing? It is easy to see what someone else may *fear*. It is not so easy to see our own. Take a moment to do the work before you turn to the next page to discover what these cases identified as their *fear*.

I can tell you it took Jeff two full sessions to find his. He said it by mistake, at first, and wanted to take it back. Amy said hers before I could explain the fact we were looking for her *fear*. Mitch's *fear* will surprise you. When I am presenting this material to a large group of leaders, Erik's is typically the easiest for the group to identify. Erik, himself, struggled a bit, but it was more of the fact that I was asking him to speak about a *fear* (any *fear*) out loud. Again, mine was easy for me, but you might not be able to readily identify it.

Identify the *fear(s)* you have for your M-L-S-S and then turn the page to discover what each of our friends identified for themselves.

	Phase 1 - A specific area that I would like to change to improve my leadership, myself, etc. (Be very specific)				
	Jeff	**Amy**	**Mitch**	**Erik**	**David**
	I need to listen to the ideas of others.	Being a stronger leader by saying *no* sometimes.	I need to lose 50 lbs.	Become a leader who is a *risk taker*.	Quit trying to fix people.
	Phase 2 – What do I need to do to impact Phase 1?				
	More of:	**Less of:**	**Stop doing:**	**Start doing:**	**Stop doing?**
By doing these things I can better accomplish my Phase 1 challenge	Give those who come in and talk with me or meet me in the hallway my undivided and full attention.	Worrying about what others think about me.	Eating at fast food restaurants.	Something I have never done before.	Looking at others as though they have a problem.
My big **FEAR** that prevents me from doing the above is:	If I listen to them, they will actually have some good ideas.	Others will think I don't care about them.	I will look small or skinny	I will fail at it.	But what if they **do** have a problem?

Jeff really did struggle with this. He kept fighting the *fear* aspect of it, but eventually started to tackle the work with a little more intentionality. At one point he blurted out, "*Maybe I fear they will have better ideas than I have?*" He wanted to take it back. I would not let him.	Amy was right on top of her *fear*. She thought this was a major breakthrough for her. She was not really having difficulty saying "no." She was *fearing* how others would interpret her thoughts about them if she said to them, "*No!*"	Mitch was not embarrassed about his *fear* and was quite quick to identify it. He added, "*I don't want to look skinny!*" Then he mentioned an Olympics swimmer he went to college with and said, "*You see that guy! Look how skinny he is. I don't want to look like that!*"	As stated, Erik had some issues with the word *fear* in and of itself. But he did recognize that the major area stopping him from trying something new was the *fear* he would fail at it and that would be a bad thing. His subconscious kept asking, "*What if I fail?*"	My thoughts were simple. I could not stop looking at people as though they had a problem because in my *mindset,* I had a *fear* that they might have a problem. Others said, "*Stop looking at people like they have a problem.*" But I kept saying, "*But what if they do?*"

As you read these responses, remember, like you, they are finding a *fear* for each M-L-S-S part of the exercise. That is the intriguing work here. As clients work through this aspect of the matrix, they often begin to see a theme about the *fear* they identify. That will be especially true when we return to Bill, Julie and Ken from the prologue. If you have named your *fears*, do you see a theme? I have a life law that states *what's in the well comes up in the bucket*. This law applies here. Let's say you have in front of you a well full of the same water (your *thought river*). What would happen if you dipped four buckets into that well, each bucket identified separately as a *more of*, a *less of*, a *stop doing* and a *start doing* bucket? What would be inside each bucket? Since the well contains only one type of water (the water of your *thought river*), each bucket would contain what was in the well. All four buckets would contain water from the same source. Don't be surprised if your *fear(s)* simply flow from the same place, from the same well. Remember, we *fear* what we believe will prevent us from reaching or achieving our *purpose/commitment*. It all comes out of the same well. That doesn't mean we don't have any divergent thoughts or fears. But as we dig deeper into why we might *fear,* we might begin to see a theme all flowing from the same *thought river*.

So, how did you do for your work? Are you digging deeper? How did you do at identifying Jeff, Julie, Mitch, Erik's and my *fear*? This is work that can only be done as we respond to the statement: The big **FEAR** that prevents me from doing my M-L-S-S work is _____!

Let's move to Phase 3 of our matrix. This is such an exciting phase! Up to this point, we have been identifying some real struggles in our lives. We completed an identifying exercise that was really a confessional booth, and we completed an exercise that made us face what most people don't even talk about: *Fear*! It is time to move into a more positive and pivoting part of the matrix. This is where we begin to identify *why* we are thinking about something the way we are thinking. Here is Phase 3:

			Phase 1 - A specific area that I would like to change to improve my leadership, myself, etc.		
			(Be very specific)		
	Jeff	**Amy**	**Mitch**	**Erik**	**David**
	I need to listen to the ideas of others.	Being a stronger leader by saying *no* sometimes.	I need to lose 50 lbs.	Become a leader who is a *risk taker*.	Quit trying to fix people.
	Phase 2 – What do I need to do to impact Phase 1?				
	More of:	**Less of:**	**Stop doing:**	**Start doing:**	**Stop doing?**
By doing these things I can better accomplish my Phase 1 challenge	Give those who come in and talk with me or meet me in the hallway my undivided and full attention.	Worrying about what others think about me.	Eating at fast food restaurants.	Something I have never done before.	Looking at others as though they have a problem.
My big FEAR that prevents me from doing the above is:	If I listen to them, they will actually have some good ideas.	Others will think I don't care about them.	I will look small or skinny	I will fail at it.	But what if they do have a problem?
	Phase 3 – What is my purpose/commitment that I am holding on to that makes me fear the above areas of my M-L-S-S?				
The reason I fear this is because I am *committed to*:					

So, what *purpose/commitment* would cause these five individuals to *fear* doing their M-L-S-S work? That is the question we must answer. How would you respond if you were each of them? What would your thoughts be as to their *purpose/commitment*? Go back to the previous page and record what you think they identified.

Here are their responses:

	Jeff	Amy	Mitch	Erik	David
Phase 1 - A specific area that I would like to change to improve my leadership, myself, etc. (Be very specific)					
	I need to listen to the ideas of others.	Being a stronger leader by saying *no* sometimes.	I need to lose 50 lbs.	Become a leader who is a *risk taker*.	Quit trying to fix people.
Phase 2 – What do I need to do to impact Phase 1					
	More of:	**Less of:**	**Stop doing:**	**Start doing:**	**Stop doing?**
By doing these things I can better accomplish my Phase 1 challenge	Give those who come in and talk with me or meet me in the hallway my undivided and full attention.	Worrying about what others think about me.	Eating at fast food restaurants.	Something I have never done before.	Looking at others as though they have a problem.
My big FEAR that prevents me from doing the above is:	If I listen to them, they will have some good ideas.	Others will think I don't care about them.	I will look small or skinny	I will fail at it.	But what if they do have a problem?
Phase 3 – What is my purpose/commitment that I hold to, that makes me fear the above areas of M-L-S-S?					
The reason I fear this is because I am *committed to*:	I am committed to being the idea person in our organization.	I am committed to showing people I care about them and want the best for them and will do things for them.	I am committed to being big and strong.	I am committed to being successful in whatever I do.	I am committed to being *available* to help those who have problems.

Let's take a brief look at each of these. But first, ask yourself this question: Do these *purpose/commitment* statements sound negative or positive, as they stand on their own merit? If you were interviewing someone and you asked them to tell you an important *purpose/commitment* that they hold to be true in their lives, and they responded by saying:

I am committed to being an idea guy in an organization!

I am committed to caring for others and showing them that they are important to me!

I am committed (as an NFL player) to be big and strong!

I am committed to never failing!

I am committed to being available to help others solve their problems!

I think if you heard those from a potential candidate you might want to hire for a job, you might think all five would be a great hire. These are good *purpose/commitment* statements for anyone in life. (This is part of the challenge on the change matrix. We are starting at the top to consider first what we would like to change about ourselves. But the thing we want to change is often hindered by the very great *purpose/commitment* statement of our lives.)

Let's just add a few thoughts to each of these five and why this is their commitment:

The reason I fear this is because I am committed to:	I am committed to being the idea person in our organization.	I am committed to showing people I care about them and want the best for them and will do things for them.	I am committed to being big and strong.	I am committed to being successful in whatever I do.	I am committed to being available to help those who have problems.
Some further thoughts:	Remember, the superintendent who originally hired Jeff wanted an *idea person*. Every teacher from the high school who was on the interview team wanted Jeff's idea *mindset*. It was the new superintendent who struggled with Jeff's need to be the *idea guy*.	Remember, Julie is now an elementary principal. Wouldn't you want a person committed to caring for others to fill that role?	Remember, Mitch was an NFL football player at one time. Would this not be a good life *purpose* and/or *commitment* if you wanted to play in the NFL?	Remember, Erik was an up-and-coming leader. He had been promoted several times to be the lead in this tool and die shop. Would it not make sense to have this *purpose* and/or *commitment* in that field?	Remember, I was told to stop helping others. But, if I pulled away and, yet, someone had a problem, what would that mean?

We want to do what we are committed to. We fear anything that might prevent that commitment. If I had started each of these entire case studies with this *purpose/commitment* statement first, you would have a different opinion of each of these five people. This Phase 3 step should be a positive statement. Our *purpose/commitment* is a positive aspect of our lives. It carries all of who we are as people. So, when others ask us to *more of, less of, stop doing,* or *start doing* something, and we perceive one of those will go against this powerful *purpose/commitment* statement, don't be surprised if we recoil.

But let's move on to Phase 4. In Phase 4, we are going to identify the bases for our *purpose/commitment*.

	Phase 1 - A specific area that I would like to change to improve my leadership, myself, etc.				
	(Be very specific)				
	Jeff	**Amy**	**Mitch**	**Erik**	**David**
	I need to listen to the ideas of others.	Being a stronger leader by saying *no* sometimes.	I need to lose 50 lbs.	Become a leader who is a *risk taker*.	Quit trying to fix people.
	Phase 2 – What do I need to do to impact Phase 1				
	More of:	**Less of:**	**Stop doing:**	**Start doing:**	**Stop doing?**
By doing these things I can better accomplish my Phase 1 challenge	Give those who come in and talk with me or meet me in the hallway my undivided and full attention.	Worrying about what others think about me.	Eating at fast food restaurants.	Something I have never done before.	Looking at others as though they have a problem.
My big FEAR that prevents me from doing the above is:	If I listen to them, they will actually have some good ideas.	Others will think I don't care about them.	I will look small or skinny	I will fail at it.	But what if they do have a problem?
	Phase 3 – What is my *purpose/commitment* that I hold to, that makes me fear the above?				
The reason I fear this is because I am committed to:	I am committed to being the idea person in our organization.	I am committed to showing people I care about them and want the best for them and will do things for them.	I am committed to being big and strong.	I am committed to being successful in whatever I do.	I am committed to being available to help those who have problems.
	Phase 4 – What is the core belief and value and passion that drives this *purpose/commitment*				
The reason I am committed is because I **believe**:	I believe people who have ideas can discover great things.	I believe people need help and I am committed to providing that help.	I believe you must be big and strong to be the BEST.	I believe in getting things right, to standards.	I believe that no one should ever lack help for their problems.
The reason I am committed is because I **value**:	The journey of looking for something new.	Serving others.	Being the Best. Excellence.	I value an achievable mark of being accurate.	I value transforming lives

The reason I am committed is because I am **passionate** about:	Discovering a new idea to help kids learn.	Helping others get what they need when they need it.	Performing at my best every day.	Putting things in order the right way.	I am passionate about being available to help others transform.

Where would these types of *thought rivers* come from? You can see, if you hold to these *mindsets*, why they might have trouble making the changes they are being asked to make. The challenge in Phase 1 is our *gap*. The work in Phases 2-4 is our *analysis*. But we still need to go a little farther to start to *bridge the gap*. Did you outline the *belief, value,* and *passion* on your analysis of yourself?

Let's dig a little deeper and add Phase 5. You tell me what you think the answers might be for the following archetype story behind these test case illustrations:

	Phase 4 – What is the core belief and value and passion that drives this *purpose/commitment*				
The reason I am committed is because I believe:	I believe people who have ideas can discover great things.	I believe people need help and I am committed to providing that help.	I believe you must be big and strong to be the BEST.	I believe in getting things right, to standards.	I believe that no one should ever not have help for their problems.
The reason I am committed is because I value:	The journey of looking for something new.	Serving others.	Being the Best. Excellence.	I value an achievable mark of right.	I value transforming lives
The reason I am committed is because I am passionate about:	Discovering a new idea to help kids learn.	Helping others get what they need when they need it.	Performing at my best every day.	Putting things in order the right way.	I am passionate about being available to help others transform.
	Phase 5 – What archetypal imprint story are these beliefs, values, and passions based upon?				
My life story is best described by this archetype(s)					

So, what archetypal story best fits Jeff? Julie? Mitch? Erick? Me? The archetypes are going to assist us in *bridging the gap* we have discovered for each of these five case studies. In a moment, I will give you the back story for each person listed in this work. The key will be to see if we can identify their imprint stories with the archetype material, which we did so much work on in Part 2 of this book. Return to pages 67 and look at the archetypes again regarding their *belief, value, passion, purpose/commitments* and *fear*. As you look it over, how would you identify our test case studies with an archetypal imprint? Also, how would you identify your own story comparing the work you are doing with what is listed on those pages?

Here are the actual responses for each of our test case individuals:

	Phase 5 – What archetypal imprint story are these beliefs, values, and passions based upon?				
	Jeff	**Julie**	**Mitch**	**Erik**	**David**
My life story is best described by this archetype(s)	Seeker and Creator	Caregiver and Lover	Warrior and Orphan	Ruler and Orphan	Magician and Sage
	He wants ideas to create new ways to help kids learn.	She wants to help others and not damage her relationship with them in the process.	He wants to succeed and avoid the dangers of being weak.	He wants things done right and he knows what is right. He sees danger in doing things wrong.	I want to transform others and I know what they should look like at the end.

You can see how each of these individuals are completely fitted for the roles they either played or are playing. If you were hiring them for the jobs they fill, you can see that this is the *best-fit* candidate for the job. Understanding someone's *archetypal* imprint gives us an analysis that they can not only do the job they are hired to do but will be motivated (*engaged* and *responding*) and *passionate*, as well. Again, if I had started at this end of the matrix, each of these individuals would have looked different in your mind. If you were using this approach for hiring someone, you probably would be starting at this end, Phase 5, and not at the beginning, Phase 1. Knowing someone's archetypal journey allows us to see what they are passionate about, but also what gaps they may have. Very few people can, on their own, *bridge the gap* created by this imprinted story of their lives. Very few people even want to discover their *gaps*. Regretfully, the gaps typically come to life as we are actively being asked to do something in our roles that simply don't fit our life imprints. *How you are primed determines the direction you are aimed.*

Where could these stories have developed for each of these individuals that it would produce such a *thought river*? What events produce these *mindsets*? What could possibly have brought them to this type of thinking? Let me introduce you to Phase 6 of our matrix.

	Phase 5 – What archetypal imprint story are these beliefs, values, and passions based upon?				
	Jeff	**Julie**	**Mitch**	**Erik**	**David**
My life story is best described by this archetype(s)	Seeker and Creator	Caregiver and Lover	Warrior and Orphan	Ruler and Orphan	Magician and Sage
Summary of the archetype impact:	He wants ideas to create new ways to help kids learn.	She wants to help others and not damage a relationship with them in the process.	He wants to succeed and avoid the dangers of being weak.	He wants things done right and he knows what is right. He sees danger in doing things wrong.	He wants to transform others and knows what they should look like at the end.
	Phase 6 – Where did the story come from? Do I need the story today? Do I need it tomorrow?				
PAST Where did this come from?	When I was in high school the junior class needed to come up with an idea for the senior Prom. I came up with the idea and that was the beginning of my "idea" career.	I was the first born in my family and responsible for taking care of five brothers and sisters. My mom and dad went through a divorce, and I was responsible to take care of the family. I was raised as a Catholic to do good works and help others.	When I was in junior high my coach said if I gained 20 pounds, I might be able to start in high school. I did. My high school coach told me the same thing if I wanted to be recruited by Michigan. I did. Bo told me the same thing if I wanted to be drafted in the NFL. I did! I was!	When I was younger my dad had a big emphasis on high grades and doing the best job in school. He didn't want me to fail. (The irony here is that his dad hired me to coach him. He still didn't want him to fail after he was away, in his own job field.)	When I was younger a man in our church sexually assaulted me. When I went to my pastor for help, he blew me off. I swore that day that I would never do that to someone. I will *always* make myself available. (Go back and look at the first words on my purpose statement on the wall of my office on page 61.)

PRESENT Where is it needed to today?	Everywhere I have been since high school has rewarded me for my ideas. I have my current position because I am an idea person.	I was hired because I take care of people and I have been promoted everywhere I have been because of my ability to take care of people.	I am currently in the Realtor field, and we put our pictures on our business cards and billboards. We are very "visual" oriented. (People view me as an ex-NFL player.)	In my current leadership role, the culture is a culture that says, "take a risk." However, anyone who took a risk in the company and failed, lost their job.	In my present life I see a value in helping others but realize it is not "if" I help them but "how" I help them. It is still important and imperative to be there for them.
FUTURE Where can I use it today?	To simply drop the desire and capability to help others come up with ideas would not be good for my career.	Where I am now, I must take care of people and that characterizes my job.	I am worried that I might be putting the focus on the "visual" too high on my list and too much of a focus for my family.	If I want to be promoted where I am and if I want to have a good relationship with my dad, I can't fail in this leadership position.	If I want to be available to help others that doesn't mean I have to help them the *way I think* they *should look at the end.*

As you read through these stories, you can see where the initial imprints come from. These stories are real and talk about how these individuals developed their *mindsets*. But how do we *bridge the gap* created from the desired change in Phase 1, to the stories in Phase 6 (especially seeing how these stories have really been seared into their subconscious)?

This brings us to Phase 7, the last and final phase.

	Jeff	Julie	Mitch	Erik	David
Phase 7 – How do we *Bridge the Gap*?					
Step #1 **(Strength or Shadow?)** Am I using the archetype in a strength or shadow way?	Jeff is using these archetypes in a partially, shadow way. The archetypes can be used for a self-journey, but they can also be used to foster Seeking and Creating among others. That is as equally as valuable.	Julie is *enabling* her staff. She is not helping them. She is hurting them. Someone who helps does not just *give* you something.	Mitch was not using his *warrior* when we met. Not in the way he did in the NFL. His relator work cut into his workout time. He didn't need to just eat less, he needed to also work out more.	Erick was using both the *Ruler* and the *Orphan* on the shadow side. He had a misguided definition of failing. He needed to learn that failing is not, not trying. He needed to learn that failing is stopping after you fail.	I was using the *Magician* on the shadow side. Rather than transforming others (my ex-wife) I was manipulating others to be what I thought they should be.
Step #2 **(Archetype alone or more?)** Am I using the archetype in balance of another?	He needs to balance these two with the Sage – teaching others how to Seek and Create.	She needs to balance the *Caregiver* with the Warrior and *help* her staff learn accountability.	He needed to bring in the *Ruler* and structure his day to include work outs. He eats to fuel workouts.	He needed to bring in the *Seeker* and the *Innocent* into his life. They both would give him insights into the possibility of new things he could perfect.	I needed to bring in the *Ruler*, create some life laws that I would not violate (see addendum 1). I needed to create (*Creator*) tools that would help others change themselves the way they wanted to change.
Step #3 **(Archetype to bridge the gap?)** What archetype story do I need to create in my *thought river* to create a *bridge* to accomplish Phase 1?	He needs to realize he would listen to them if he was trying to solicit their ideas so he could teach them to *seek* and *create* on their own. This will allow him to be valuable in the organization. But he would have to *listen* to them first to teach them how to turn their ideas into tangible outcomes.	By building a relationship with them (*Lover*) centered around accountability, she will both strengthen the relationships and truly be a *caring* leader. She needs to, as the saying goes, teach them to fish, not just give them a fish.	He needs to find a way to pursue his workouts by valuing them over other priorities. He was seeing the danger (*Orphan*) of not working out, but not doing anything about it (*Ruler*).	By not doing anything new Erik was failing his dad. His dad wanted him to be successful. Creating a story where he adventures out of his comfort zone would be a stronger story than being locked in and only perfecting the status quo.	By bringing in the *Ruler* and *Creator*, I quit trying to *fix* people and instead pivoted to providing tools to people so they can *fix* themselves (like books … like this book).

92

The ability to look into ourselves so that we can see the *gaps* we have is a vital part of maturity in our leadership. The ability to help others do this same work is mandatory for our leadership. We can't simply be content to tell people what we need them to do. Leadership today is understanding our team so that we can *bridge* who they are with what we need them to do. Of course, this can't happen for every job we do in our work-a-day world. Most people apply for jobs that they believe will fill their buckets. They see a job that interests them based upon their *thought river*, their *prime*. It is when their roles and responsibilities begin to expand outside of what they thought they were going to be doing that we might find more and more *gaps* between their mindset and their work product. Great leaders need to be able to lead their staff through the necessary changes in their mindset to help their team identify areas of their thinking that might be preventing them from achieving what is required of them.

To summarize, let's look at our five case studies again, but through the following lens:

	Jeff	Julie	Mitch	Erik	David
What was their *cognitive anchor*?					
What was their *assumed constraint*?					
What was their *ochyroma*?					

How would you answer these questions for our case studies? You should now know enough to be able to identify these. We walked through the *gaps* created by these three areas. But it would be great to identify them so that we can keep them in our minds as we do more work. What would you put in each box? Create this same table for your self-reflection work. What would you put in your boxes?

Before you turn the page, take a moment to really think about these five one more time.

Here is what we discovered when doing this work with them. Some of what you are about to read comes from additional work with them, but these responses were summaries of their own personal journey through the matrix:

	Jeff	Julie	Mitch	Erik	David
What was their *cognitive anchor?*	He believed that his only source of value was coming up with ideas. Only his ideas were valuable.	She believes that she must help others to get them to connect with her and value her.	Bigger is better!	Leaders can't fail.	I need to be a fixer of all things that hurt.
What was their *assumed constraint?*	He assumed he didn't have time to listen to other people's ideas when they have no clue what a good idea looks like anyhow.	She can't hold people accountable because they won't value her if she does.	He doesn't have time to work out anymore because he must work at a job. (Unlike the NFL where you are paid to work out.)	If he can't do something exactly right the first time, he won't do something. So, he doesn't want to try something new. He might fail.	I can't say no to someone who needs help. If I do, I will look like the pastor who didn't help me. I don't want to look like that.
What was their *ochyroma?*	When he is in a tight spot he runs to the *Seeker* and *Creator* archetypes to succeed. That means *he* is doing something, not listening to people.	When she is in a tight spot she will run to *Caregiver* and *Lover*. That means her helping others and not requiring others to do something for themselves.	When he is in a tight space, he needs to do something, (like working out), not stop doing something like (stop eating). The entire mindset to *stop* doing something is a struggle.	When he is in a tight space, he will do what he has always done so that there is less risk and more guaranteed outcomes.	When I am in a tight space, I try to transform someone, or something. However, I had to learn to transform myself first and only help others transform if, when and how they want to transform.

When we find a *gap* in those we lead (or ourselves), the key to *bridge the gap* is to unfold their life story and help them rebuild a new story. We must take time to learn their old story and help them retain the parts that are still essential. But we have to help them unlearn the parts that are causing a *gap* and learn a new story that will be more practical, useful and comparable with their current situation. Archetypal imprints give us a practical and beneficial way to create a new story. This new story can flow into our *ever-changing and moving historical river of past experiences and accumulated knowledge.* That new river will begin to produce new *beliefs, values, passions,* and *purpose/commitments.* It will also create new *fears* in us, however. That means the work never ends. The *mindset* we currently have is constantly changing. The question is whether the changes are intentional (based upon *gap analysis*) work or simply by chance. It is more successful when we do so by intentional *gap analysis* using archetypal imprints to do so.

One last install of our case subjects:

	Jeff	Julie	Mitch	Erik	David
How did it come out for them?	Jeff created a ten-step process to help his staff take their ideas (*Seeker*) to fruition (*Creator*). He found that he was highly valuable to his organization for helping them create ideas and finish them. Years later his superintendent informed me we created a monster. He is always asking everyone what step they are on regarding his 10-step process.	Julie would eventually retire from that same school as an elementary principal. They did not want to see her go. She now consults. When others would ask her for something she would say, "Let me *HELP* you ask me that in a different way so that you can get what you need by doing and not by simply asking."	Mitch would leave his position with his partners to start his own business as a business broker. He would make time each day to work out and get his fitness back. He is now my business advisor and looks like the days he played. He is not in that condition, of course, but his workouts pay off. I think the beer is gone from his menu but not always the burger and fries.	Erik had to tell his dad that the thing that was holding him back was his dad's constant desire to define what success was for him. He eventually did start his own business. He failed! Then he started it again and at last report is thriving.	David had to stop trying to fix everyone. He started to refer to himself as an executive leadership coach. The word coach means you take people from point A to point B. He now creates tools to help others get from THEIR point A to THEIR point B. If they don't like the tool, they don't have to use it. He just creates the tools (like the one you just learned).

Summary of Parts 1-3

Let's close these first three parts off by returning to Bill, Julie and Ken. I am simply going to give you their entire change matrix and how this work is applied so that you can see how what you just worked through can be used to close their *gaps*. It should be noted that this type of work is long, tedious and messy. It is not easy, or necessarily healthy, to put it in boxes and columns and rows. But the work is profitable if you take your time to do the work. It is healthy to examine our lives. You may or may not agree with Socrates' statement that *an unexamined life is not worth living*. Taken at its face value, it resonates with what this book is about. I don't think those who live *unexamined* lives, however, suffer from a lack of worthy living. But for the leader who wants to develop and grow their staff and fill the gaps they have in their organization; Socrates' words give us much to think about.

Take a look at how the processes would unfold for Bill, Julie and Ken because they willingly *examined* their lives:

	Bill	Julie	Ken
Phase 1 - A specific area that I would like to change to improve my leadership, myself, etc. (Be very specific)			
	I need to stop worrying when I make mistakes.	I need to stop helping everyone to bail them out.	I need to be creative – not be so rigid.
Phase 2 – What do I need to do to impact Phase 1			
	More of:	**Stop doing:**	**Start doing:**
By doing these things I can better accomplish my Phase 1 challenge	I am going to start taking corrections and examine what I am doing.	Stop immediately stepping in when I see someone needing help.	Start doing more out of the box thinking and things.
My big FEAR that prevents me from doing the above is:	Someone will disapprove of me and use it to slow my progress and/or career.	The work will not get done in the best way that it can be done, and we will have to do it again.	What if I come up with the wrong solutions and/or thinking?
Phase 3 – What is my purpose/commitment that I hold to, that makes me fear the above areas of M-L-S-S?			
The reason I fear this is because I am committed to:	I am committed to being seen as someone who does things the right way and/or the best way.	I am committed to making sure the organization gets the work done and done right so we don't have to repeat work.	I am committed to doing the job I was given (HR) and making sure the processes are correct and measurable.
Phase 4 – What is the core belief and value and passion that drives this *purpose/commitment*?			
The reason I am committed is because I **believe**:	When I don't make mistakes, I am valuable to the organization. (When I keep up with excellence.)	If you don't do it right the first time you have to do it again, so do it right the first time.	Creativity is not often seen as achievement.
The reason I am committed is because I **value**:	Approval and/or connection.	Excellence.	Achievement.

The reason I am committed is because I am **passionate** about:	Making sure my connections with others are not damaged by my mistakes.	Getting it done and getting it done right.	Getting something done that is measurable and shows value.
	Phase 5 – What archetypal imprint story are these beliefs, values, and passions based upon?		
My life story is best described by this archetype(s)	Lover and Warrior	Caregiver, Warrior, Ruler	Warrior and Ruler (but wants to have more Creator)
	He needs to be connected and valued by those around him by making sure he performs in exactly the right way.	She needs to come in to help others, but not to simply help them but also to assure that the work is done right, and the organization won't fail.	He can't be creative because he believes being achievable trumps creativity. Creativity is dangerous since it is not as measurable as his daily work.
	Phase 6 – Where did the story come from? Do I need the story today? Do I need it tomorrow?		
PAST Where did this come from:	Bill was disciplined for not reading fast enough and keeping up with others. He was often challenged to stay in step based upon the opinions and/or directions of others.	Julie was made to do everything over again if she made a mistake. It was never *good enough*.	Ken was told by his ex-boss he was not supposed to be creative. He was told to focus on the technical side of his job and leave the creative side up to her.
PRESENT Where is it needed to today?	He can use this story as motivation to help him strive for excellence, but because he desires it and not because others desire it; based upon his terms, not the terms of others.	She needs to strive for excellence but allow others to make mistakes, coach them and help them learn from their mistakes.	He needs to continue to do his best in the technical side. That has advanced his career. But he needs to re-learn that creativity can and should be part of that work and the role he plays.
FUTURE Where can I use it today?	He needs to keep the excellence aspect of his story but re-imagine the *doing it for others* part of his story.	She needs to retain the desire to do the best you can but give herself and others grace to make mistakes. She needs to pull others into the work to help them grow and teach them to overcome any mistakes that might happen.	He needs to continue to advance his desire for excellence, while at the same time find a way to incorporate his creative desires into his role as Director of HR.

	Phase 7 – How do we *Bridge the Gap*?		
Step #1 **(Strength or Shadow?)** Am I using the archetype in a strength or shadow way?	He is using the *Lover* and the *Warrior* in the shadow side. The *Lover* should establish relationships, but not be based upon his performance (*Warrior*). If he has to prove himself to keep the relationship whole, he really doesn't have a relationship.	She is using the *Warrior* in a way that focuses on perfection and the *Caregiver* is not actually helping others. She is more enabling than she is caring for others.	His *Warrior* Seems to be dialed in correctly, but his *Creator* Is dormant and subservient to the *Warrior/Ruler*. The *Creator* should be able to live without reaching the excellence and perfection the *Warrior* and/or *Ruler* demands.
Step #2 **(Archetype alone or more?)** Am I using the archetype in balance of another?	Bill would do well to add to his *Thought River* the *Magician* archetype. The *Magician* will give him some insight on how to transform these moments he feels like he failed into moments of growth and maturity.	Julie would do well to change her *mindset* about her role as a leader. She thinks her job is to get things done. But her role as a leader is to grow and mature her staff through the work and the mistakes, so that they can get things done. This calls for the *Magician* archetype.	Ken needs to realize that the *Creator* can produce measurable and achievable results. To just create for the sake of creating is not the definition of the *Creator* on the strength side. If he combines the *Creator* with the *Ruler* archetype, he can structure and design something that fits his role as a HR leader and advances his organization.
Step #3 **(Archetype to bridge the gap?)** What archetype story do I need to create in my *thought river* to create a *bridge* to accomplish Phase 1?	He needs to add the *Magician* and learn how to convert mistakes to triumphs. He needs to incorporate the *Seeker* and see that there are new ways to establish value for himself in the organization, not just connecting with others (*Lover*).	She needs to find a way to be the *Caregiver* but not enable. She can do that if she takes on more of a coaching role in her leadership and less the *Ruler* role. She can do that by pouring *Magician* stories into her *Thought River*, not just *Ruler* stories.	He needs to pour the *Creator* into his *Thought River* and allow himself to create, fail, correct, and excel. He is so fixated on the thought that someone he admired and gave him his job was, at the same time, limiting his capacity to use his passion: Creativity.

These stories of Bill, Julie and Ken are real parts of their lives. After examining their behaviors through the lens of this matrix, they found a new way to behave that allows them to live in their *belief, values, passions*, and *purposes/commitments* and still adjust their work style to fit those roles they were given. You can too! But you will have to change your *Thought River*: Your *ever-changing and moving historical river of past experiences and accumulated knowledge*. Until you pour more into that river and filter what is coming out, you will have *gaps*. You can *bridge the gaps* when you know where the *gaps* came from.

Hand-Off

(David hands-off to Lori)

There are many places and scenarios where *Gap Analysis* can benefit both organizations and leadership. To assist in the application of Parts 1-3, my colleague, Dr. Lori Tubbergen Clark, will present to you Part 4. One of the areas where *Gap Analysis* can benefit leaders, organizations, as well as a potential employee is in the hiring and onboarding process. Lori is going to focus on that sweet spot of a deeper application.

I met Lori years ago while doing work for her organization. While leading her team, she incorporated the previous material in Parts 1-3 for both her leaders and followers. The culture of her organization was both enhanced and equipped as she wove this material into the collective mindsets of her staff and work. She has, however, not only used the material, but she has also richly expanded the impact.

You are about to read how *AP Analysis* can better qualify candidates for your staffing positions and assist as you work all the way through the onboarding process to even further coach new hires for success. As they fulfill their technical skills and reveal their mindset needs, *Gap Analysis* can enhance them for their organizational role. Lori will show you how using this material will not only ensure you have the best work, it will give you confidence of the best fit.

Enjoy and be willing to be challenged as Lori supplies a framework to make necessary changes in your own day-to-day staffing needs.

PART 4
Best-fit strategies to organizational staffing

"People are not your most important asset. The right people are.

Get the right people on the bus… and the right people in the right seats."

–Collins, J. (2001). *Good to Great*. Random House Business Books.

Have you ever had a bad hire? Did you discover after the fact that you hired the wrong person or that your new hire was obviously in the wrong seat on your organization's bus? If so, you are not alone. Wrong hire rates are high and cost you time, money and damage your culture. If you rely heavily on a personal interview to make your hires, it raises your likelihood of wrong hires. Personal interviews have been a leading strategy to select the best candidate for a position. Most of us have been through the "tell me about yourself" and "where would you see yourself in 3 years" grilling for a prospective job. Traditional, unstructured interviews alone cannot predict a candidate's performance or their potential effectiveness and have anecdotally proven to be totally flawed and even a detrimental practice laced with subjectivity and bias.

While not exact, the United States Department of Labor estimates the average cost of a bad hire is up to 30% of the employee's first-year earnings. That means that an employee that you've is-hired for a $60,000 annual salary will cost you about $18,000 in time and expenses associated with onboarding and training the wrong hire, terminating the wrong hire, and then re-hiring and repeating the onboarding and training process with their replacement.

Time and expenses associated with a wrong hire are easy items to quantify. Think of the other high costs to your organization that are harder to quantify, such as hours spent posting positions, reviewing resumes, and interviewing candidates. Think of the hours that leaders spend managing the poor performance of a wrong hire and the drain on the rest of your team from their poor performance. Not to mention the significant negative impact that a wrong hire can have on team morale, mental and emotional health, and organization culture, or the risk of increased legal fees to handle claims that might result from the termination of the wrong hire.

Consider the following real-life hiring horror stories that stemmed from using a traditional interview process in isolation; stories that illustrate the need to include more data and gap analysis in the selection process. Names and identifying details in the following have been changed to protect the privacy of individuals.

"Horror Story: The Culture Catastrophe"

During the personal interview with candidates for the open principal position at the elementary school, the Superintendent found a candidate who rose to the top. Bailey had prior experience in administration, a compelling presence, and convincing examples of systems and structures previously developed and implemented. The district's elementary school needed a leader who could give some structure to building operations, something the former leader lacked. Nine months into the position as a school principal, the Superintendent began hearing concerns about Bailey's leadership from the elementary staff. They reported that their new leader placed a huge emphasis on rules at the expense of serving students, citing several examples. Teachers were complaining that they had no latitude to do their jobs and lived in fear of their new principal's inflexible rules. When veteran staff attempted to have difficult conversations with Bailey about the concerns they had about their deteriorating building culture, the principal avoided the conversations and seemed more interested in self-preservation and the power of the principal position than serving students. Worse yet, their new leader seemed to favor the newer staff, who quietly followed the rules and did as they were told, over the more veteran staff, who challenged what they perceived as a new bureaucracy that at times seemed thoughtless to the needs of students.

Bailey was not operating by the core values of compassion and collaboration that the school district fundamentally practiced regarding how staff would work together to achieve their mission. Staff wondered if the superintendent even shared their district's core values with their new leader during the inadequate onboarding process. They perceived Bailey as destroying what was once a positive school culture due to the lack of flexibility, poor communication, and a host of new policies, structures and rules that were too much and implemented too fast. Bailey was creating procedures and structure that were needed but created it in a non-collaborative vacuum that was destroying a once positive school culture. Their new leader was a culture catastrophe. The superintendent was disappointed and bewildered by his selection of Bailey as the new principal. How could things have gone so wrong so quickly with Bailey? Bailey had been so charismatic and confident during the personal interview, had a great resume, and had excellent examples of systems previously created and implemented.

Lesson learned: Organization culture matters if you want high staff engagement and retention, and how candidates will impact your culture is paramount. Cultural considerations should play a key role in how you post, recruit, select, onboard, and support new leaders.

The superintendent used a traditional job posting form for the building principal position, advertised the position on various media, and completed the hiring process in isolation during June, not involving school year instructional staff in the process to avoid disrupting their summer vacations. The district had neither onboarding processes to support Bailey in understanding the district's core values and the boundaries of positional authority nor a coaching plan to support their newest leader. Bailey was left to work in isolation in the elementary building, making decisions in a vacuum, leading to a poor succession plan and minimally effective leadership at best. Not to mention the staff that were quickly looking for new seats on a different bus.

Before reading the following gap analysis, return to Part 3. Using the change matrix below, what would you assess is Bailey's belief, value, passion, purpose/commitment and/or fear? Return to Part 2 and review the twelve archetypes. Based upon the above narrative about Bailey's story, which archetype do you think that Bailey would score highest? Which archetype do you think Bailey would score lowest? What archetype imprint story do you think would help Bailey improve? What would an improved fit look like? Use the table below to record your reflections.

			Change Matrix			
Belief	Value	Passion	Purpose/Commitment	Fear	Archetype(s) Bailey is currently displaying	Archetype story that would help Bailey improve

Gap analysis: The Pearson Marr Archetypal Indicator (PMAI®) would have brought attention to the fact that Bailey expressed a very high Ruler archetype and expressed very little Magician archetype. With this knowledge, the superintendent would have clearly defined the limits of Bailey's authority in the position of the building principal, giving Bailey as much autonomy as possible while setting expectations for modeling the district's core values of collaboration and compassion. With an understanding of Bailey's archetypal imprints, the superintendent, with the support of an executive coach, would have supported Bailey's focus on the valuable contributions to the workplace using his confident and responsible Ruler strengths and coach him to use Magician tools to find win-win solutions to problems and to resolve conflict that happens with change processes, rather than exhausting staff the staff and creating rules and procedures that were not student-focused. With a coach supporting Bailey's leadership growth, there would have been a chance at balancing high Ruler tendencies with the Magician archetype tools, and rather than acting alone in creating rules for the elementary building, true transformation of the elementary school would have been possible, and staff may have appreciated the needed structures to be able to operate efficiently and effectively to the benefit of staff and students.

Look back at the Change Matrix that you completed and compare it to the one below:

Change Matrix						
Belief	Value	Passion	Purpose/Commitment	Fear	Archetype(s) Bailey is currently displaying	Archetype story that would help Bailey improve
The school should have order.	Methodical rules to bring structure.	Bringing organization to the staff and school.	Bringing order to a school that was once in disorder.	Conflict created by staff not operating within an established system.	Ruler	Magician

"Horror Story: The Oblivious Binge Watcher"

Joe spent a significant amount of time searching for his new executive assistant. The executive assistant would be the first person that visitors encountered entering the office, and due to the large amount of highly detailed contracts and technical agreements that the assistant was responsible for executing, Joe needed his new assistant to have not only a keen eye for details but also a friendly unifying presence in the office. His current executive assistant was retiring after working with Joe for nearly 20 years, and Joe was dreading trying to replace his current dynamic assistant. She took care of everyone and everything in the office and was incredibly competent. Joe worried about nothing in her realm, and she would be tough to replace. Joe decided that in addition to the personal interviews that he routinely did, he would also give candidates a written assessment to test their performance on detailed tasks. After he completed the personal interviews and the candidates completed the performance assessment, Joe made his selection. Adrian would be his new executive assistant. Adrian had experience with all job duties, an outstanding written performance-based assessment that indicated high skills and great attention to details, and a very pleasing personality during the interview. Joe was confident Adrian was going to be the perfect fit and a good replacement for his retiring executive assistant.

Adrian's first day on the job affirmed that his new executive assistant was not only a quick learner but also friendly with office staff and visitors. On Adrian's second day of work, Joe noticed his new assistant was watching a movie on the work computer while reviewing and editing personnel contracts. Joe immediately asked Adrian why a movie was playing on the desktop computer while simultaneously editing important contracts. Adrian informed Joe that multitasking was easy for the younger generation and not to worry about a thing. Joe clearly told Adrian that watching movies during work time on the work desktop was not allowed and that 100% focus was needed for him to be confident that the technical work was completed to his high standards. Problem solved, Joe thought. Adrian is cranking out great quality work, completing all assigned tasks and then some, and performing all job responsibilities well.

On day three in the position, Joe noticed Adrian's phone perched on top of the desktop, and Adrian was engrossed in a Netflix series on the phone with air pods securely blocking out office sounds, visitor's voices, and his voice, while simultaneously responding to email. Joe was in disbelief after yesterday's conversation. Joe thought perhaps he was not clear, and the next conversation ensued.

Joe: "What's with the distraction on your personal technology today, especially after our conversation yesterday?"

Adrian: "Just finishing up a Netflix series I started yesterday."

Joe: "I told you yesterday that watching movies at work was not permitted and that I need your focus on your work."

Adrian: "You told me that I couldn't watch movies on the work desktop. I switched to my phone, which works better anyway because my air pods block out everyone else in the office."

Joe: "Let me be clearer. You may not watch movies during work time on any device. You need to focus on your work and building relationships with the rest of the team in this office."

Joe thought he was crystal clear on the expectation this time.

On day four of Adrian's tenure, Joe once again found her air pods in her ears, one eye on the Netflix series on her phone and the other on her work computer screen, completing contract amendments—work that requires complete focus and no mistakes. Joe didn't need to say anything. Adrian popped her air pods out and said, "I'm almost finished with the series. And I'm almost finished with these contracts. They'll be to you a day earlier than you wanted them."

On Friday—the last day of Adrian's first week on the job—after Joe's three attempts in three days to resolve the problem, late in the afternoon, Adrian was back to binge-watching the latest addictive series begun the previous night. Adrian failed to take any feedback from Joe and failed to interact with anyone in the office, so Joe terminated Adrian at the end of one very long week and gave Adrian lots of time to binge-watch Netflix. Binge watcher lasted one week on the job.

Lesson learned: Always do reference checks! Joe skipped reference checks. Adrian's skill level exceeded his expectations, and gave an outstanding personal interview. After all, reference checks often are not very objective, and sometimes all they do is verify employment. Bias-filled reference checks have never had an impact on any of Joe's hires, so he skipped them. Joe failed to ask anyone on the reference list about the characteristics that were most important to the position---that Adrian was helpful, supportive and caring about the workplace culture.

There is no guarantee that Joe would have received valuable information about Adrian's work ethic and difficulty receiving feedback from reference checking, but it is a small investment in time to request the name(s) of someone that candidates have worked with in the past and ask three simple questions to check for alignment of what the candidate is selling you on their resume and telling you in the interview. Questions that most former work colleagues will most likely answer include: "What time frame did you work with the candidate?" "What was the candidate's job responsibilities when you worked with them?" "Would you rehire or recommend the candidate for this position?"

Had Joe taken one more step and completed reference checks, perhaps he would have learned that Adrian has a history of binge-watching entertainment at work. Before reading the following gap analysis, return to Part 3. Using the change matrix, what would you assess as Adrian's belief, value, passion, purpose/commitment and/or fear? Return to Part 2 and review the twelve archetypes. Based upon the above narrative about Adrian's story, which archetype do you think Adrian would score highest? Which archetype do you think Adrian would score lowest? What archetype imprint story do you think would help Adrian improve?

Change Matrix						
Belief	Value	Passion	Purpose/Commitment	Fear	Archetype(s) Adrian is currently displaying	Archetype story that would help Adrian improve

Gap Analysis: The Pearson Marr Archetypal Indicator (PMAI®) would have indicated that Adrian's assessment revealed that the Caregiver and Lover archetypes would have had lower scores. Although during the personal interview, Adrian indicated that helping and supporting other members of the office team would be a priority and that building compassionate relationships was important, those contributions did not materialize in the workplace. With Adrian's PMAI® data in hand, Joe would have been in a better position to frame scenario questions during the interview process that would have revealed that Adrian may have difficulty in an office where helping, supporting, and building relationships was required.

Joe would have also discovered that Adrian's data revealed a less developed Jester archetype expression. Armed with this data, maybe Joe would have probed more during the interview or onboarding process regarding Adrian's irresponsibility, lack of accountability, and ethical issues.

Look back at the Change Matrix that you completed and compare it to the one below:

Change Matrix						
Belief	Value	Passion	Purpose/Commitment	Fear	Archetype(s) Adrian is currently displaying	Archetype story that would help Adrian improve
Time at work should be fun.	Enjoyment	Driven by having joy in life.	Making work enjoyable.	Taking things at work too seriously.	Jester (Shadow)	Caregiver Lover

"Horror Story: Deer in the Headlights"

The new Human Resources (HR) Director held a position with an identical title in her former community. Relocating due to a spouse's job transfer, Ryley took the lateral move into what appeared to be a similar position based on the job posting. Not excited about the relocation or learning a new job, Ryley hoped that leaving the HR Director position in what had been home for 15 years and transferring to an HR Director position in their new community would be an easy transition and a gentle learning curve. Based on the job posting, it sounded promising for an easy transition.

The CEO that hired Ryley hoped for the same. After all, it was the busiest time of year in the HR department, and it was critical that the position be filled quickly. Finding a candidate with prior experience who held a similar position in a different company seemed the logical choice. The former veteran HR director left the organization with just two weeks' notice due to a family tragedy, and the position needed to be filled quickly. What luck to find Ryley, who was looking for a lateral move to the community.

Upon arriving for the first day on the job, Ryley found that the organization did not have a formal onboarding process and was left to figure things out with the small existing team of support personnel. The organization also lacked formal, written policies and procedures to provide guidance on how to handle common workplace situations that filtered into the human resources office. Ryley had little direction on what was expected, what was appropriate, and what was not appropriate, which created confusion from day one. When questions began coming about the code of conduct, personal cell phone use, dress codes, etc., there was no guidance, and HR staff provided conflicting institutional knowledge. Ryley noticed issues were not handled with consistency. Staff coming to the HR office for guidance received different guidance from different staff members on the team.

Ryley's former employer not only had well-documented policies, procedures, and guidance documents, but they also had an employee handbook that assured consistency and fair treatment of staff. Ryley was adept at following written policies and assuring staff adhered to them, but creating new policies and a system in which they could be implemented was a skillset lacking in Ryley's wheelhouse. Based on the job posting, this is not what Ryley signed up for or expected of the new position. The organization operated in individual vacuums, and Ryley had no support from other leaders or a clear path forward. Confusion increased. Inefficiencies ensued. Staff was not happy. Ryley floundered. Worst transition to a new position ever, thought Ryley.

Lesson learned: Don't assume. Accurate job postings are key for candidate recruitment and a critical step in selecting the best candidate. Matching a candidate's actual talent and skills with the competencies required and assuring the match through scenario-based evidence or a performance-based assessment would have uncovered the mismatch of job requirements and Ryley's current skills level. Onboarding is important. Left in isolation, Ryley continued to flounder.

Change Matrix						
Belief	Value	Passion	Purpose/Commitment	Fear	Archetype(s) Ryley is currently displaying	Archetype story that would help Ryley improve

Gap Analysis: The Pearson Marr Archetypal Indicator (PMAI®) would have indicated that Ryley's assessment revealed that the Creator archetype would have had the lowest score and the Lover archetype was among the highest. Although Ryley's resume indicated prior experience as a Human Resources Director, Ryley had no experience in creating policies, procedures, guidance documents, etc. Ryley was skilled at implementing a well-developed HR system but had no interest and got no energy from trying to develop a system from square one. Armed with Ryley's PMAI® data, the CEO would have been in a better position to frame scenario questions during the interview process that would have revealed that Ryley may have difficulty in an organization that needed system development work and departed from the status quo that Ryley desperately wanted to hold on to from the former position.

Look back at the Change Matrix that you completed and compare it to the one below:

Change Matrix						
Belief	Value	Passion	Purpose/Commitment	Fear	Archetype(s) Ryley is currently displaying	Archetype story that would help Ryley improve
Created to connect	Relationships	Holding onto to the system they value.	Holding on to people and systems that they value.	Anything that damages what they love.	Lover	Creator

Data-based gap analysis improves hiring success. Personnel costs are often an organization's largest operating expense, and mistakes in hiring have a significant impact on the budget and worker morale. There are no perfect candidates, but an improved data-based process and gap analysis during the selection process can enhance your hiring process and diminish your odds of wrong hires. The United States Bureau of Labor Statistics (2020) data show that, on average, organizations lose 6% of their staff annually due to poor performance (involuntary turnover), and another 13% of staff leave of their own volition. During a period of staff shortages for critical positions, turnover due to mis-hiring and/or poor onboarding practices, along with the resulting damage, should be analyzed and proactively addressed through gap analysis in the posting, screening, interviewing, selection, onboarding, and coaching processes. Organizations see benefit from adding objective data and bias control to their otherwise subjective interview process.

Part 4- Section 2

In Part 1 of this book, you learned about cognitive anchors—anchors in your mindset that powerfully influence how you think. Perhaps *"It's time to fill our vacant position"* is quickly followed with the cognitive anchor: *"We need to schedule personal interviews with applicants."* That cognitive anchor will provide familiar comfort but may also lead to false assumptions, and during a candidate selection process may not end with the best hiring result. What cognitive anchor(s) in your hiring process do you need to consider unlearning or rewriting? Are your cognitive anchors contributing to bias in your hiring process?

Traditional hiring and high wrong hire rates set the stage for why leaders in organizations need to change their mindset and implement objective, data-based practices to get the best fit for critical positions. With some tweaks and additions to the traditional selection process, the likelihood of selecting the best fit and increasing hiring success is realized. Figure 1 below illustrates a recommended process that rewrites the hiring process and includes gap analysis steps to improve your process, as well as enhancements to control bias.

The eight components of the new and improved selection process illustrate the value of investing in data collection and gap analysis and will improve your candidate selection process.

Figure 1. Phases of a New and Improved Selection Process to Select Best-Fit Candidates

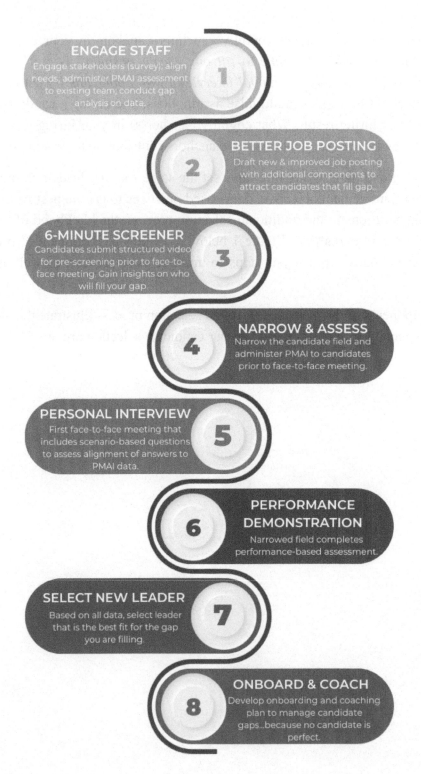

Traditional approaches often result in hiring for a candidate's likeability during a personal interview, tending toward charisma rather than competency and best fit. You will notice that this recommended process does not throw the personal interview away but rather incorporates the personal interview into a more data-based selection process. Most candidates can prepare very well for interviews and are able to project the image that they think the employer wants to see. With so many online resources, candidates have practice interview questions at their fingertips to help them prepare and can memorize the "look for" answers, resulting in a stellar performance during a personal interview.

You may be thinking, *"Eight steps—that will take too much time." "A personal interview is how we have always hired." "Eight steps to hire someone will take a lot of hard work."* Each of those thoughts are assumed constraints--beliefs that limit your selection process. You will find value in acknowledging and reframing your assumed constraints about your current interviewing and selection process. Flip your assumed constraints into a statement that will lead you to proactive, positive action: *"Investing time in collecting data and analyzing gaps will help select the best candidate and save time and money in the long run."*

Phase 1: Engage Stakeholders and Assess Leaders

What are you and your team looking for in your next hire? Do you need a candidate who shares the beliefs and values of your organization, or do you need a candidate with different, more diverse beliefs but who can align with your values while at work? As the leader, do you really understand your team, and have you clearly identified the gap you need to fill in the hiring and selection process?

The process begins with engaging stakeholders in the selection process. Stakeholders include leaders in the organization, staff who will be co-workers of the new hire, partners, and constituents with whom the new hire will work. If the new hire is a school building principal, consider engaging students in this initial step of the selection process.

In short, engaged employees who are involved in and enthusiastic about their work and workplace are retained, productive, and effective; have low rates of absenteeism; and experience higher well-being. Based on their 2021 survey, Gallup reports that just 34% of U.S. workers surveyed are engaged at work. Obviously, the pandemic plays a factor in this data, but that number is not improving. The survey measures several workplace elements, including employees' level of agreement about clarity of expectations, opportunities for development, their opinions counting at work, having the right materials and equipment, the opportunity to do what they do best every day, and a connection to the mission or purpose of their organization. Gallup also observed a sharp drop in the percentage of employees who strongly agree that their employer cares about their overall well-being. Employee engagement is foundational to improving the well-being and resilience of staff because well-being includes components of communication, caring, development, involvement, and collaboration. These components set the stage for developing trust in the workplace culture, which is essential when addressing overall well-being. In his book <u>Trust! Using Archetypal Language to Repair Broken Trust</u>, Hulings (2023) says, "When conflict hits a community, satisfaction is hampered, production is diminished, and teamwork finds itself under siege. And in all of this, the worst aftershock of unhealthy conflict is the loss of trust." Phase 1 is not only an engagement phase and a data-collection phase but also a trust-building phase.

The data is compelling. Engaging stakeholders, listening to their opinions, and finding out what really matters to them relative to the new leader is important to overall selection success. Hiring a new leader without feedback from the team will not lead to the most successful result. The new leader will either make or break the team, and allowing team members a voice in the vetting process demonstrates that you value the team. Asking for feedback from the team in the hiring process paves the way for a smooth onboarding process and builds a culture of trust.

Surveying stakeholders to gather feedback that identifies leadership characteristics, skills, behaviors, and actions that the new leader must possess to assure employee workplace satisfaction; identifying perceived challenges that the new leader will need to address; and determining actions the new leader will need to take to drive continuous improvement is an important step in the engagement process. Design your survey to be brief, ensuring neutral language in the survey questions. Allow for open-ended responses to receive genuine feedback from stakeholders rather than Likert-scaled questions. For example, genuine feedback from staff can be garnered with a survey with questions such as, "From your perspective, what do you believe are the most immediate challenges we face that our new leader will need to tackle?" "What do you believe are the two or three long-term challenges our organization will need to address in the near future?" "What leadership background and skills will be needed to address those issues?" "What beliefs and values do our leaders need to demonstrate each day to fill our current gap?" The data that you generate from responses to these types of open-ended questions will be much more valuable than a question such as, "On a scale of 1 to 5, rank the importance of a leader's ability to inspire others to reach a common goal." See Addendum A for sample stakeholder survey questions.

Gap analysis: After the data from stakeholders is collected, analyze and prioritize the feedback data to use throughout the rest of the process. Identify the gaps between stakeholder data and your expectations for the new leader. Alignment between your expectations for the new hire and the expectations and wishes of those who will work with them is vital not only for the best-fit hire but also for more engaged stakeholders. Sharing the results of your data collection and gap analysis will contribute to building a dedicated team, a culture of trust, and positive public optics.

Option to control bias: Opt for anonymity in stakeholder surveys to reduce the risk of survey response bias. Stakeholders are more likely to give direct, honest feedback when they have the option of submitting anonymous responses. Also, invite **all** stakeholders to complete the survey, not just a select few, to control sampling bias. Send the survey with an email campaign; place a link to the feedback survey on your website; offer a QR code to take the survey; and even consider face-to-face meetings to collect feedback data from stakeholders. Offering multiple methods to submit feedback assures access to all stakeholders.

Concurrent with collecting stakeholder feedback, Pearson Marr Archetypal Indicator (PMAI®) data for leadership team members is collected as a tool for our gap analysis work and will inform the recruiting and selection process. The PMAI® instrument is a scientifically validated archetype assessment tool. It provides a path to self-understanding and a better understanding of leadership teams. (See Part 2.) Once teams are aware of the archetypes that are active, they can better decide how and when to use them, which ones are not present—a gap that needs to be filled by a new candidate or archetype tools that need to be developed. Dr. Carol Pearson, author and thought leader in an archetypal narrative, describes it this way (www.storywell.com):

PMAI® results can enable you to make choices that fulfill you as you begin to see your motivations more clearly. Deeper than that, with this information, you can recognize that your archetypes serve as lenses through which you observe the world, which can tip you off to what you are not seeing because it gets filtered out. This, in turn, can improve your relationships as you gain a readily accessible way to notice what archetypes are active in others and thus understand why they think differently than you do. Your results also can inform you about your low-scoring archetypes, which can help you comprehend why you may have trouble getting motivated to accomplish certain tasks or have a difficult time dealing with certain people when the work or the interaction with them requires an archetype that does not come naturally to you. Understanding which archetypes generate energy within a group then can be used in...leadership and organizational development, and employee recruitment and retention to support outcomes that are good for the organization and its stakeholders..."

By identifying current leadership team behaviors, motivators, and influencers active in the workplace culture through PMAI® data and where there may be gaps, candidates can be better matched to an organization for better fit and positive results. Comparing candidate results with the results of the leadership team will determine complementary archetypes, identify strengths and gaps in the team, and help team members appreciate differences in people.

The table below illustrates a leadership team profile generated by the results of the individual leader's PMAI results. The team profile focuses on the three highest-scoring archetypes (inner allies) of each leader and the lowest-two-scoring archetypes. The result provides a collective picture of the current team and a method to identify archetype gaps.

SAMPLE LEADERSHIP TEAM ARCHETYPE PROFILE					
	Archetype #1 (Highest)	Archetype #2	Archetype #3	Second Lowest Archetype	Lowest Archetype
Leader A	Idealist	Caregiver	Ruler	Warrior	Seeker
Leader B	Magician	Revolutionary	Warrior	Jester	Ruler
Leader C	Realist	Caregiver	Jester	Sage	Creator
Leader D	Realist	Magician	Caregiver	Revolutionary	Seeker
Leader E	Realist	Caregiver	Lover	Jester	Sage
Leader F	Caregiver	Warrior	Idealist	Seeker	Realist
Leader G	Idealist	Sage	Lover	Creator	Revolutionary
VACANCY	?	?	?	?	?

The three highest-scoring archetypes are those that a leader senses familiarity with and will feel skilled in the attributes and talents the three highest archetypes represent. These three highest archetypes provide feelings of authenticity, potential, and energy and represent what the leader is focused on and most interested in at the moment in time they completed the assessment. The two lowest-scoring archetypes are sometimes called "blind spots" and represent qualities that are a low priority for that leader or attributes that simply are not in their wheelhouse. (Blandin, K., Marr, H., Person, C., PMAI Manual, 2021)

In the sample leadership team archetype profile above, notice that none of the current members of the leadership team display strengths in the attributes and talents that the Seeker and the Creator archetype represents. Only one leader assessed Sage in their top three archetypes. If this leadership team is on the cusp of visioning the future five years (Creator) of their organization, or if they are searching for new opportunities (Seeker) that are research-based best practices (Sage) to grow their services, they might be interested in speaking with a candidate who has talents in these areas.

Being aware of the strengths and gaps of your current leadership team may be useful in asking gap analysis questions in searching for your best-fit candidate when you find a vacancy on your leadership team.

Gap Analysis Questions:
1. Which archetypes are <u>not</u> represented in the collective team's highest-scoring archetypes (Inner Allies)?
2. What impact might the absence of these archetypal tools have on the leadership team's ability to accomplish the organization's vision, mission, and goals?
3. Are there specific archetypal tools that you prefer the new leader (vacancy) display as strengths (in their top three)?
4. How fixed or fluid is my current team's profile? (Remember, archetypes are fluid in our lives. What we are today, may not be what we are tomorrow. If your current team (as pictured above) has *blind spots*, they may not be a permanent lack of vision. As you bring on a new hire, however, this is the key moment to augment your team with someone who might display these *blind spot* archetypes naturally.). But, if your team is *fixed* in their archetypal maturity, a new hire who can display these less preferred archetypes will increase the maturity of your team.

Before moving to Phase 2 of the process, consider these questions at the completion of Phase one of your selection process:

- Are your expectations for the new leader and the stakeholder feedback data aligned?
- Based on your stakeholder data, how well has your organization articulated the vision, mission, and values of your organization?
- What are the leadership strengths and gaps in your current team?
- What gap should the new leader fill?
- Have you controlled for bias?

To recruit the candidate that is the best fit for your organization, data collection and analysis are key to the rest of the process. What is the gap that exists between the skills, behaviors, and characteristics of your current team and those skills, behaviors, and characteristics required by your organization to reach its goals? The next 7 phases will assist in filling your gap and lead to your success. See Addendum F to record the results of your PMAI® leadership team archetype profile that highlights the strengths and gaps of your leadership team and complete the gap analysis processing questions.

BETTER JOB POSTING
Draft new & improved job posting
with additional components to
attract candidates that fill gap.

Phase 2: Better Job Posting

The job posting that you publish is often the first impression of your organization and the first impression that a candidate gleans of your organization. What kind of impression are you making? Generally, a job posting includes the job title, position summary, position responsibilities, and qualifications. These components are important. However, if your posting does not specifically recruit for the gap you need to fill based on the data from phase one of the process, you may not receive the best-fit candidates you are seeking. Does your job posting clearly articulate what you are looking for in your next hire? Consider a new and improved job posting with additional components to attract candidates to fill the gap you've identified. Some questions to consider as you evaluate your current job postings:

- Does your job title match the job responsibilities?
- Does your job posting use clear, concise language? For example, rather than saying the position "will cross-functionally interface across multiple departments", use "will collaborate with," which sounds friendlier.
- Does your job posting include the vision and mission of your organization?
- Does your job posting include the non-negotiable core tenets or guiding principles that your organization has adopted and expects all staff to adhere to in their work?
- Does your job posting include the beliefs, values, passions, and purpose of the organization as a whole?
- What are the specific behavior and character traits you are seeking that reflect your expectations and stakeholder feedback?
- What competencies, skills, and talents are needed for a candidate to be successful in the position based on your expectations and stakeholder feedback?
- How does your posting attract candidates that you want and discourage candidates that you prefer to apply?
- Is there a specific archetypal presence for your leadership team that you are seeking to fill in this position?
- What archetypal vocabulary should you use to communicate the above areas? See a sample archetype lexicon word bank in Addendum G.

These are important questions to consider as you evaluate your job postings. Use data analyzed during phase one to assure specific requirements for candidates and of the position are integrated into your job posting so you have a great blueprint. A well-crafted job posting will increase your probability of receiving excellent candidates. Consider adding photos to attract attention with links to your online presence, social and other media, location-based lures that are attractive for relocation, and even testimonials from current staff describing why your organization is a great place to work.

Control for bias: Have you considered any biases in your job posting? Use a gender-neutral phrase such as "the candidate" rather than "he" or "she." Scan your job posting for words that may discourage female applicants, such as "chair***man***" or "work***man***ship." Check for outdated language such as "maternity leave" and rather use "parenting time off" to appeal to a broader candidate pool.

With data from engaged stakeholders and an improved job posting, you are ready to post your job and recruit a candidate pool for your position.

Phase 3: 6-Minute Screener

How can you authentically screen many candidates in a short amount of time? The 6-minute Screener is a pre-interview screening video. Rather than beginning with the traditional route of reading resumes and ranking applicants to determine who might be a promising candidate with whom you'd like to speak, consider adding a pre-interview screening video to your process. A pre-interview screening video is time-effective, inexpensive and provides an opportunity for employers to meet potential candidates prior to a face-to-face formal interview. Asking candidates to send you a 6-minute video answering two or three structured questions about themselves and the position allows employers great advantages. Carefully choose what questions you ask for the 6-minute screener that encourages candidates to talk about their ideals. Their answers will tell you if their ideals align with the core tenets of your organization. For example, if your organization has core tenets of *collaboration* and *accountability*, one of the structured interview questions that you could ask candidates to respond to in their screening video might be, "*Describe a successful team project you have led, how you organized and led your team, and what your contribution was to the project?*"

Consider using the 6-minute screener to explore the candidates' beliefs, values, passion and purpose (commitment and/or fear). Recall from the previous section that:
- *Belief* is a conviction we hold true even in the most critical moments of life.
- *Value* is the weight of importance and/or priority of collective beliefs.
- *Passion* is the energy we feel, demonstrate, and/or express as we live out our beliefs and values.
  Gap analysis in this phase is about discovering how well a candidate's beliefs, values, and passions align with your organization and with the position they are seeking. The following questions can be used for the 6-minute screener to determine alignment:
- *What are your core beliefs or convictions relative to this position that will influence your motivation and decision-making?*
- *Which of these beliefs do you most value and why?*
- *What about this position are you passionate about that would fuel energy for you each day?*
- *What actions will we see in your leadership that will reflect your beliefs, values, and passions? (purpose)*

The employer can also get a sense of a candidate's communication skills and personality by asking a generic open-ended question such as, *"Why are you the best fit for this position?"* A candidate's word choice in their 6-minute video screener can provide archetypal information to you. (Reference the Word Bank in Addendum G.)

Video screening is a less subjective method to conduct initial screenings when compared to reading through resumes and ranking candidates. All candidates are given the same structured questions with the same time limit, which reduces bias in the initial selection process. This step in the process also allows employers to screen many potential candidates in a shorter amount of time.

Employers can analyze candidate responses on several criteria. Did they articulately answer the structured questions you posed? Did they highlight their qualifications and why they are your best candidate based on the job posting? Did they reference your organization's vision, mission and/or core values and how their beliefs, values, and passion align with them? Is the candidate using positive, professional language that is appropriate for the position you have posted? Are you hearing any slang? Did the candidate take the opportunity to showcase their personality? Can you detect a fixed or fluid mindset with their word choice? What keywords and phrases are they using that give you clues to archetype strengths? Do you have any inclination as to if the candidate will fill the gaps you identified? Did the candidate use all six minutes allotted? The following checklist (Addendum H) can be utilized when evaluating candidate 6-minute screeners:

Criteria for Analyzing Candidate 6-minute Screening Videos or Audio Submissions	
Did the candidate articulately and completely answer the structured questions you posed? Evidence:	YES or NO
Does the candidates, beliefs, values, passions, and purpose align with your organization? Are there gaps to fill? Evidence:	YES or NO
Did they highlight their qualifications and why they are your best candidate based on the job posting? Evidence:	YES or NO
What keywords and phrases are they using that give you clues to archetype strengths? Evidence:	YES or NO
Can you detect a fixed or fluid mindset with their word choice? Evidence:	FIXED or FLUID
Did they reference your organization's vision, mission and/or core values and explain how they align with them? Evidence:	YES or NO

Is the candidate using positive, professional language that is appropriate for the position you have posted? Are you hearing any slang? Evidence:	YES or NO
Did the candidate take the opportunity to showcase their personality? Evidence:	YES or NO
Do you have any inclination as to if the candidate will fill the gaps you identified? Evidence:	YES or NO
Did the candidate use all of the 6-minute time allotment? *(Quality candidates generally can fill the entire 6 minutes.)* Time: _____	YES or NO
What archetypal language did you hear? *(Reference word bank that corresponds with each archetype in Addendum B.)* Does the language you heard align with the archetype(s) you are seeking for this position?	YES or NO
Other Evidence:	

Control for bias: Consider implementing a 6-minute audio screener rather than a 6-minute video screener. Bias blindfolds are removed as soon as a leader sees a candidate. Like it or not, images can trigger unconscious bias. Using audio screeners rather than video screeners can control unconscious biases such as age, race, cultural background, perceived attractiveness or not, wardrobe choices, video background choice, etc.

Phase 4: Narrow and Assess

Following the analysis of the 6-minute screener data, and a review of resumes, the candidate field can be narrowed to those with whom you would like to meet in person. Prior to a face-to-face meeting and formal personal interviews, the Pearson Marr Archetype Inventory (PMAI®) is administered to each candidate. A candidate's PMAI® assessment is reviewed along with the leadership team's PMAI® assessment results from Phase 1. This gives a great picture of the team's collective strengths and motivations and insights into relationships and culture.

PMAI® results can assist in seeing a candidate's motivations more clearly and can serve as a lens through which they currently observe the world and what a candidate might currently be filtering out. The results also can inform about low-scoring archetypes, which can frame personal interview questions. Now that you have a team profile and candidate profiles, you have the necessary data to complete a gap analysis.

Gap Analysis

Gap analysis will not guarantee that you will find the perfect candidate because all candidates and every organization have gaps. By identifying the gaps, letting the gaps inform your hiring process, and creating coaching scripts to manage and fill the gaps, your likelihood for success will increase. This approach will find the best candidate and augment candidate gaps and your organizational gaps to assure success.

Phase 5: Personal Interviews

Consider the face-to-face personal interview a competency interview. In addition to the traditional questions that are commonly asked, frame interview questions that allow you to validate if the candidate's answers match what you identified as required competencies in your job posting. Ask questions to determine how the candidate handles challenges and tasks in their previous position. Listen for answers where candidates share specific examples where they demonstrated the needed skills and behaviors you've identified. Consider adding scenario-based questions structured to discover a candidate's fixed or fluid mindset. Scenario-based questions will also allow the employer to consider the cognitive framing of the candidates and aid in understanding a candidate's *thought river* and what has been formed in it and by it. Listen carefully to candidate responses to validate the alignment of answers to their PMAI® assessment results.

For example, when asked to describe their leadership style and a candidate responds that they are a nurturing, servant leader that is self-sacrificing and excels at supporting their team with compassion. However, their PMAI® assessment indicates a very low score in the Caregiver archetype, indicating a misalignment between the candidate's answer and the assessment data. Employers would want to dig deeper into that answer because the data cannot be validated by the candidate's response.

The table below provides sample archetype scenario interview questions to consider during personal interviews.

Archetype Scenario Interview Questions to Determine Competency	
Idealist (Innocent)	We want leaders who are optimistically resilient, and who build a culture of trust and a positive mindset in students, staff and families. Give me an example of how you've dealt with challenges/frustrations while maintaining trust and positivity? Describe how you have positively contributed to a team.
Realist (Orphan)	Describe a time when you proactively identified and addressed a problem at your current workplace. Describe a difficult decision that you resolved in a past workplace.
Warrior	We are looking for a leader who demonstrates a desire to excel. Give an example of a time that you've worked to excel. What have you embarked upon in the past year that has led to continuous improvement? Have you ever completed a difficult task as part of a team? Tell us about it. What would you consider your biggest workplace achievement? Describe three of your strengths and how they will impact your leadership. What do you believe your greatest barrier will be to being successful in this position? What action will you take to act upon that?
Caregiver	Give us an example of how you have supported and grown your team members, building capacity in them as leaders. What strategies did you find most successful? How and when would you provide positive feedback to staff? Describe what it would look like. How will you take care of your people? How would you promote diversity, equity, and inclusion in our workplace?
Seeker	We need a leader who is consistently looking for opportunities, trying new things, and learning from their mistakes. Do you consider yourself to be a risk taker? Give an example of when you seized a new opportunity and what you learned.
Lover	Describe the relationship you want to cultivate with your new colleagues. What actions would you take to cultivate those relationships? Share a time when you adapted and committed to a major change within your organization and built consensus among stakeholders. Be specific. OR What do you love about your current position? What excites you most about this position?
Revolutionary (Destroyer)	Staff members you lead throughout a new project disagree with your vision and implementation plans because it is a big departure from how they've previously functioned. What specific steps would you take to address their concerns? (Leadership and decision-making skills) Describe a significant change you've made in the workplace and how you implemented it, and how you dealt with resistors.
Creator	We need a leader who is forward-thinking and can articulate an inspirational vision and practice shared leadership for the continuous improvement for our organization. If we were setting goals for next year, what would they be? We want leaders who can envision the schools of tomorrow, ones that align with more engaging and flexible learning environments. If you could create the ideal learning program, what would it be like? Describe a time when you used creativity to solve a problem in the workplace.

121

Ruler	Imagine you need to implement a new system with which you do not have much experience. What steps do you take to gather information and ensure successful execution? What kinds of things do you think your staff will need clear expectations for?
Magician	Identify two growth areas you will be working on in this position and explain how you will go about that growing process. We want leaders who are not afraid to challenge the status quo and are able to stretch the thinking of others. In what ways have you or will you challenge your colleagues' thinking and be a positive catalyst for transformation? After several corrective conversations, and other supports, a staff member you supervise is still well below performance expectations. What is your next step?
Sage	Tell us about a time that you did data-based, long-range, big-picture planning and share your approach. We are looking for a leader who demonstrates lifelong learner and is honing their skills, using a variety of professional resources to consider new best practice approaches. What learning have you embarked on in the past year that has led to continuous improvement or a new approach? Why was that your focus?
Jester	What have you found fulfilling in your current position? What do you think you will enjoy most about this position?
Cognitive Anchors	What have you learned in life that you want to consider unlearning?
General	When work has piled up, and you are facing a project deadline with your team, what is the first thing that you do? Describe a time when you successfully handled conflict in the workplace.

If you chose not to use the recommended questions regarding a candidate's beliefs, values, passions, and purpose during the 6-minute screener phase, include them during the personal interview phase to determine alignment:

- *What are your core beliefs or convictions relative to this position that will influence your motivation and decision-making?*
- *Which of these beliefs do you most value and why?*
- *What about this position are you passionate about that would fuel energy for you each day?*
- *What actions will we see in your leadership that will reflect your beliefs, values, and passions? (purpose)*

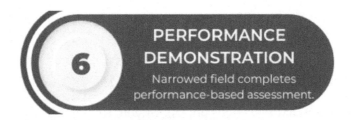

Phase 6: Performance or Demonstration Assessment

Some candidates are great at personal interviews, but observing them in action performing part of the job is a valuable component in which to invest. Many have witnessed the perfect, polished interviewers who won a position, and when they got to the real work of the job, they choked. The performance or demonstration assessment is a means to validate a candidate's **practical skills by requesting they perform job-specific tasks**. Think of it as a "job audition." This validation step protects the organization from the perfect, polished interviewee and assures that the candidate can actually perform job competencies.

For example, if your job posting is for a Director of Communications and includes competencies for proficient writing and ease with public speaking, a performance or demonstration assessment could include a timed, written response to a prompt along with a verbal presentation with the interview team as their audience to validate the candidate's competency.

If your job posting is for a Chief Financial Officer who will lead all financial matters and competencies, including oversight of the budget for your organization, the performance or demonstration assessment could include the development of a mock department budget and the creation of a sample quarterly report to validate competency.

If your job posting is for a school superintendent who needs to lead the passage of a bond issue during the first year, the performance or demonstration assessment could include the development and presentation of the candidate's first 100 days plan of action to validate competency in what your organization needs.

Investing time to implement this extra measure of asking candidates to submit to a "job audition" is worth the validation, a wise return on your time investment.

Control for bias: The performance/demonstration assessment, in many cases, could be performed blindly. In blind interviews, the interviewer does not know the identity of the person completing the performance/demonstration assessment. This is done to protect the identity of the person being interviewed and control bias. If the performance/demonstration assessment can be implemented "blind," consider giving candidates a fair chance to show what they can do without any preconceived notions coming into play.

Phase 7: Select Your New Leader

Review the gap that exists between the skills, behaviors, and characteristics of your current team and those skills, behaviors, and characteristics required by your organization to reach its goals. Review the stakeholder feedback data, the competencies of your job posting, the screener and personal interviews, and the data from the performance/demonstration assessment. Focus objectively on the data, and based upon the data, determine which candidate fills the gaps that you identified.

Determine which gaps the candidate does not fill for you. Remember, there are no perfect candidates. Consider if the potential candidate is coachable in the areas where gaps remain. Meaning, is the candidate capable and ready to do what it takes to change, transform, or improve in areas where there are remaining gaps? Is there evidence that the candidate shares your vision, is passionate, open to change and willing to learn? If so, the candidate is probably coachable, and the gaps can likely be filled. If the answer is the opposite, you may want to reconsider your selection.

The Candidate Data Organizer in Addendum I may be a useful tool in organizing your data and analyzing gaps for each candidate as you deliberate on your final selection. When you are confident in your selection, follow your organization's human resources procedures for background checks, criminal record checks, etc., prior to extending an offer to your candidate.

Phase 8: Onboard and Coach

Filling the position is just the beginning of the work. During phase 8, the long-term work begins. We have learned that mis-hires were due to the factors found below the tip of the traditional interview iceberg—factors that simply were not even considered. The first seven phases of a data-based process to select your best-fit candidates have brought you below the tip of the traditional interview iceberg and concludes with onboarding and coaching. This phase is a critical step of the process and one that is often overlooked. Many organizations have systems to orient new staff to their organizations. They have a series of tasks that new hires complete in the human resources and technology departments, which is orientation and not necessarily onboarding and coaching.

Onboarding is more than assigning a workspace, giving access to email accounts, completing the necessary paperwork to get paid, and other required operational tasks that all new hires must complete. It is more than introducing the newest member of the team to their new colleagues. It is more than supporting the new hire as they become familiar with the work environment. It is much more comprehensive than the traditional new staff orientation day. An organization that is not thoughtful and not intentional about how they onboard and coach their newest team member is wasting the time investment they just made during the first seven phases of this process. It's worth it to continue investing in your new hire, to help them be as great as they can be, to help them bridge any gaps that will make them a greater asset to the team, and to retain leadership talent. Comprehensive onboarding and coaching systems are key to retaining the new talent you just selected.

The candidate you just selected worked to make a good first impression on you during the hiring process. Think of your onboarding and coaching process as your organization's chance to make a great first impression on your new hire. How you onboard and coach your newest team members says a great deal about your organization's culture, the workplace climate, how you treat your staff, and what your team dynamics are. Many organizations have onboarding software modules as part of their human resources departments, which is a great beginning. However, comprehensive onboarding and coaching system is individualized to the new leader and the position in which they will serve the organization.

Coaching should be at the heart of your onboarding process. Coaching was a remedial strategy used for leaders who were in trouble, viewed as a punitive punishment by some. Coaching should be viewed as a powerful, empowering gift that organizations invest in for all new leaders and as a privilege.

The coach and the CEO, in partnership with the new hire, assess gaps and leadership skills required based on data collected during the interview and selection process. Coaches work with the new leader to analyze data; write leadership goals that reflect the data; fill the identified gaps for optimal performance on their new team and in their new position; write an action plan for the first 90 days in the position; and develop a coaching plan for the first year.

An external executive coach can impartially assess and develop leadership skills that position your new leader and your team for success, intentionally bridging the gaps identified in the first seven phases of the selection process.

The material in Parts 1-3 will benefit the coaching process. Even when we do the very best we can in the hiring process, we will still discover that our *best* hire will have gaps that need to be filled in the coaching process. Discovering the gaps during the selection process will provide the most effective coaching plan. Using the material in the previous portion of this material gives us a plan of how to close those discovered gaps, to increase a candidate's performance, and demonstrate the credibility of our hiring process.

A last consideration in the onboarding process is to consider what the needs of your new hire will be based on their archetype profile. For example:

	What They Will Want In The Workplace
Idealist **(Innocent)**	The Idealist will want to feel safe in their position and to be reassured they can trust their colleagues.
Realist **(Orphan)**	The Realist will desire belonging in the workplace and a sense of job security.
Warrior	The Warrior will need to be given goals to accomplish and opportunities to develop and refine their skills.
Caregiver	The Caregiver will need to know how to find and express the care they want.
Seeker	The Seeker will know how and where to share their ideas.
Lover	The Lover will need opportunities to build relationships to people and connection and passion to their work.
Revolutionary **(Destroyer)**	The Revolutionary will want to create efficiencies in their position to achieve excellence.
Creator	The Creator will need the freedom to be creative with their vision for their position.
Ruler	The Ruler will need the responsibility to create systems or structures that create order in their position.
Magician	The Magician will want opportunities to transform individuals and/or the organization.
Sage	The Sage will need to know where they find additional places for learning.
Jester	The Jester will need to find enjoyment in their work, to give and receive joy.

When we take time in the onboarding process to think through how to match the new hire's mindset with their tasks and roles via coaching, we find that future challenges are diminished or perhaps even erased.

Conclusion:
The Power of Life's LEGO Blocks!

Have you ever played with Legos? Imagine having a pile of Legos like to the right. Could you build a tower of Legos on top of these, seen in this pile? You probably would quickly say, "Yes, I could!" That doesn't seem that difficult of a task. Legos are for building towers, so a pile of Legos would make building one rather easy. However, what if I told you that you cannot move this pile of Legos in any way before you start the building? Imagine trying to erect a tower on a bunch of Legos that are just piled like chopped wood dumped onto the ground. You, of course, would like to first create a base of Legos before you begin erecting the tower. You can't build a tower of Legos unless you first take the Legos and make them buildable. No one can build a tower of Legos on top of other Legos that are not, at first, with intentionality, laid out in a particular way to form a base for the tower.

This is exactly the issue we have been addressing in this book. You and I have **L**ife **E**xperiences that are **G**rowth **O**pportunities. Our **L**ife **E**xperiences that are **G**rowth **O**pportunities (LEGOs) are the base of our leadership tower. Our LEGOs are the foundation of our organizational cultures. The challenge that most leaders and followers face is that they don't want to take the time and energy necessary to lay these LEGOs out in an intentional manner and as a structured basis for their growth. As stated early in this book, we don't want to go deeper before we go higher. These LEGOs form our archetypal imprints. When we ignore the imprints of the past, we leave potential elements for our growth simply lying in a pile. When we fail to investigate these archetypes, we may lose a possible building block to support our leadership present and future. The archetypes formed in the past shape the leaders and followers of the present.

As we read about each person in this book, we read about their LEGOs, their archetypal imprints. They decided to take the natural pile of events from their past life and investigate them, analyze them and organize them for potential growth. That is what *Gap Analysis* is all about. It is about taking all of our collective *thought river* and finding out what we can build. In this book, we have learned that we have different types of LEGOs:

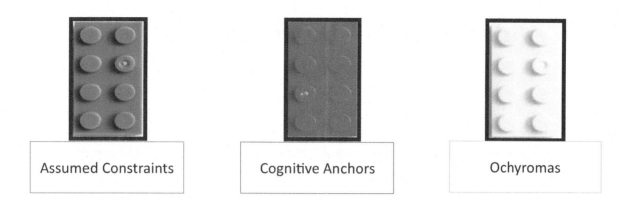

| Assumed Constraints | Cognitive Anchors | Ochyromas |

We have learned that some of our LEGOs help us, and some of our LEGOs hinder our tower of leadership. However, as we look deeper into them and begin to lay them out in orderly form, tapping into their stories, we can build our leadership and the leaders/followers around us. *Gap Analysis* is all about taking our collective LEGOs and building leaders and organizations that blend all of our life stories from interconnected fragments into sustainable structures of fulfillment that benefit all.

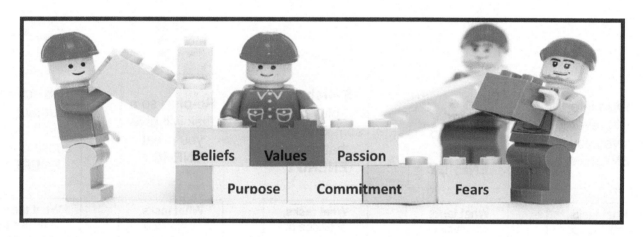

Addendum A – David's Bucket List

When attempting to live in a *purpose*-driven world, you must know what gives you energy and what sucks the energy out of you. Below are the five *buckets* I use to schedule my day. I do not take on activities based on time, availability or calendar openings. I take on projects and my day-to-day work based on these five criteria. It is never clean. It is always messy. But this is my guiding *bucket list* to keep me mostly in my energy sweet spot. The next time someone asks you to do something, join something, or get involved, ask yourself which *bucket* that request fits into. Obviously, you want everything in the first bucket. But that is just not the case. But you can't conserve your energy until you know what is killing your energy. This is a start:

Plug into whatever gives you **ENERGY**	**Cut** the plug from what sucks up your **ENERGY**	**Switch** the plug to someone else that gains **ENERGY**	**Re-plug** so a task will give you great **ENERGY**	**Structure** your plugs to limit their sucking your **ENERGY**
What tasks, activities or events give you energy?	What tasks, activities or events do you do that should simply be tossed?	What tasks, activities or events do you do that you could give to others that will give them energy?	What tasks, activities or events can you do differently so they produce energy rather than suck it out of you?	What tasks, activities or events do you do that you can't toss, transfer or change and must still do them?

Addendum B – Each Archetype's Possible Ochyroma

Archetype	Possible ochyroma	Reason it is a strength	Why it could be a prison
Idealist (Innocent)	The Innocent will run to a place where he or she believes everything is always going to work out. They just trust everything and everyone. **OCHYROMA: Believing all is well!**	Hope is a good strength to have in your life. People who live without hope can often be depressed. Running to and hiding in a fortress of hope helps us to remain optimistic in times of trouble.	When I always hope that things will work out, I can sometimes stick my head in the sand and not realize that I have a responsibility. I just assume other people will take care of it. Because I trust that things will work out so much, I am in prison because I may not see reality.
Realist (Orphan)	The Orphan typically wants to see danger and is looking for things that may hurt people. They want to be the ones who point out the danger so that they can rescue people from certain perils. **OCHYROMA: Seeing dangers before anyone else sees them!**	Looking out for danger, especially in unique times, certainly makes sense. The entire concept of an Ochyroma (a place to run for safety) is very much a fortress built by the Orphan voice.	Always looking for danger can often become a prison, because you were never free from the dangers that you may have perceived. You were locked into always having to look for danger. It never lets you out, because if you got out, you might be back in danger.
Caregiver	The Caregiver always wants to help. They're willing to be self-sacrificing, supportive, and always be the available person. They volunteer endlessly. **OCHYROMA: Helping others accomplish their goals!**	This is a strength for Caregivers, because they see opportunities that will help others move closer to their goals. They are less concerned about their own goals and more concerned about what matters to others. That is very valuable in our society.	Helping others can become a prison very fast if they don't have boundaries. They might struggle to make decisions for themselves, or fail to advocate for their own needs, because they are always worried about how it will hinder their helping other people.
Warrior	The Warrior wants to excel, to win, to secure the reward, to be battle-ready. **OCHYROMA: Exhibiting excellence in all matters!**	Being able to be excellent in everything you do is a badge of courage. People point to you as an example of how things should be done. You are a doer of things, known for not just action, but the ways in which you achieve results.	Having the pressure of getting things done correctly and in the most excellent way, every time, can be a prison. You are locked into a set of accomplishments and standards. You're never free from doing anything except the very best. When or if a time crunch occurs, it may be difficult to perform your best over and over and over.

Archetype	Possible ochyroma	Reason it is a strength	Why it could be a prison
Seeker	The Seeker views life as a journey. Seekers are always looking for something different, like their version of Nirvana. They want to find what others cannot find or envision. **OCHYROMA: Seeing what others can't even imagine!**	Seekers take us places no one else can take us. They have the ability to see a world that is better. They are able to lift us up to new heights, new adventures, new ways of thinking, and new ways of doing things.	Seekers are always looking for Nirvana. When they find Nirvana, the next morning they must pack up their tents and drive off and find it again, because they feel that what they found could not possibly be what they truly wanted. In this regard, they are imprisoned because they are never truly satisfied.
Lover	The Lover wants to embrace the past and embrace others. Lovers desire to ensure that everyone comes together passionately around a cause or goal. **OCHYROMA: Holding on!**	Lovers get juiced by bringing everyone together. They get strength from holding onto values they deem best for all. They run to this stronghold to make sure things remain the same as long as possible.	When you spend much of your energy holding on to the values that were celebrated in the past, that can quickly become a prison for a person or to the past, or both. Lovers can embrace something so hard that the thing they're embracing actually holds them back.
Revolutionary (Destroyer)	The Destroyer dismantles what is no longer effective. They want to start the first step of a revolution by taking down what is not working. **OCHYROMA: Their desire and skill set are to take things apart, and knowing this is vital if you want effective change!**	Destroyers want to make sure that their time is not wasted. When they begin to take things apart that are no longer efficient, it gives them energy to know that they are making sure people are not engaged in inefficiency.	If you get energy from taking things apart, you might, at times, find yourself dismantling things that should have been left as is. You might be imprisoned by misplaced desire to tear down structures as an end.
Creator	The Creator needs to put tangible things together, beyond ideas, stretching everyone to "build" the *instrument* that could be a product to help everyone. **OCHYROMA: Their need to build and put substance into ideas!**	Being able to point to something you created can be exhilarating, and Creators are highly valued for this vital quality. In a crisis, they want to build and endeavor to provide tangible solutions and products to address complicated challenges.	When you run to create something every time, you face the challenge of an uphill battle. To create means you must have material and resources, along with a level of approval from those you need to appease.

Archetype	Possible ochyroma	Reason it is a strength	Why it could be a prison
Ruler	The Ruler wants to put life in order, using structure, policies, and procedures to set the kingdom in order. Rulers cannot tolerate disorder and/or dysfunction. **OCHYROMA: Structure and order; being in control!**	Organizing and structuring keeps the Rulers in control of their world. When faced with challenges they run to control things; when in control, they feel safe.	Being in control of everything can be a challenge. Control is often an illusion. We can't always control the world around us. When we need to control to feel safe, we can become imprisoned.
Magician	The Magician has the need and desire to transform the world around him or her. They want to be catalysts for positive change, both individually and globally. **OCHYROMA: Transformative change!**	Seeing transformation in the lives of others can be powerful. The ability to change others' cultures and/or directions is powerful. Magicians run to this stronghold when they see challenges as opportunities.	Having a desire to change things is demanding. It can imprison a person who always feels the need to transform, because many people do not want to change; rather, they prefer the status quo.
Sage	The Sage wants to learn new things and teach others what they know. That want to pursue truth, and are often very knowledgeable, manifesting a deep need to express their knowledge to others. **OCHYROMA: Knowing everything that is important to know!**	Having knowledge is powerful. Knowing what others may not have discovered and being able to teach it to them gives Sages much value. They run to their knowledge when faced with a challenge to share what they have learned with others.	Needing to know everything can easily become a prison. Often, it is not possible to know everything. When faced with a challenge the Sage is often in a prison because they need to have the answers but can't find them.
Jester	The Jester wants to enjoy life. They need to have fun and want others to join them in the joy they create. **OCHYROMA: Enjoyment as they maneuver through life!**	When faced with challenges, Jesters create enjoyment, naturally seeking to turn sorrows and challenges into portals for joy and happiness.	Not everyone wants to party, laugh, or even smile during a challenge. Needing to have everyone enjoy themselves all the time can be a trap. There is a time to laugh, but also a time to mourn. Needing to have fun all the time can be a prison.

Addendum C – David's Life Laws

Law #1

What's in the well comes up in the bucket. (Individual character determines long-term outcomes.)

Law #2

You reap what you sow. (You can't expect to do something and not have the results show up later in your life, either for good or for bad.)

Law #3

We won't accomplish goals our habits don't support. (Goals only matter if you have the habits to support them. Modern-day goal setting can be dreaming, not habit building.)

Law #4

The whole can only be as strong as the parts. (The quality of the whole team is determined by the quality of each of the individual players.) It is not the size of the undertaking you take. What matters is the depth of character of those that you take in your undertakings.

Law #5

For every action, there is a reaction. (We do not live in a vacuum or on an island. Everything and everybody is affected by others.)

Law #6

Time is running out. (The longer you wait to improve your performance, the longer it takes to increase your productivity.)

Law #7

You get what you honor. (When you give your time, energy, resources, and attention to something, you give it an honor. Whatever you honor is what you will eventually get.)

Law #8

A nursed grudge will give birth to a bitter child. (Unresolved problems produce unwanted outcomes.)

Law #9

There is more milk than manure in a barn moment. (In the difficult situations of life (barn moments), you can either fling manure or step around it and find the milk. Where there are cows, there is manure, but if you want milk, you must focus on the cows. The key is to avoid the manure in your attempt to get the milk.)

Law #10

For every pound of criticism, there is an ounce of truth. (Mature people realize they have flaws. It is only the mature person who can take being informed by others about those flaws and will work on improving them in the context of healthy relationships.) Another way to say this would be, "I will not let the words of others determine my worth, but I will let them speak to my growth."

Law #11

Fail to ponder your path, fail to create positive growth. (Those who fail to consider how they work and lead will fail to evaluate properly and miss opportunities for growth. Fail to ponder; prepare to wander.)

Law #12

How we are *primed* determines the direction we are *aimed*. Our life decisions *often* impact the *narrative* of our lives. But the *narrative* of our lives *always* impacts the decisions we make. (Narratives that are based upon false or distorted information will often create fear, and that fear will almost always lead to destructive decisions for our lives and, possibly, the lives of others.)

Law #13

Our emotions are dictated by our cognitive framing. We often allow circumstances to determine how we feel. However, emotions can often take on a life of their own. When we *frame* the events of our lives in the right posture, we can put them into perspective. How we *frame* these events and circumstances with our mind will eventually produce the chemicals in our body that produce the emotions of our lives. It all starts with, however, how we *frame* an event.

Addendum D – Change Matrix

Phase 1 - A specific area that I would like to change to improve my leadership, myself, etc. (Be specific)				
	Phase 2 – What do I need to do to impact Phase 1			
	More of:	**Less of:**	**Stop doing:**	**Start doing:**
By doing these things I can better accomplish my Phase 1 challenge				
My big FEAR that prevents me from doing the above is:				
	Phase 3 – What is my purpose/commitment that I hold to, that makes me fear the above areas?			
The reason I fear this is because I am committed to:				
	Phase 4 – What is the core belief and value and passion that drives this *purpose/commitment*			
The reason I am committed is because **I believe:**				
The reason I am committed is because **I value:**				
The reason I am committed is because I am **passionate** about:				

	Phase 5 – What archetypal imprint story are these beliefs, values, and passions based upon?			
My life story is best described by this archetype(s)				
	Phase 6 – Where did the story come from? Do I need the story? Do I need it tomorrow?			
PAST Where did it come from?				
PRESENT Where is it needed today?				
FUTURE Where can I use it today?				
	Phase 7 – How do we *Bridge the Gap?*			
Step #1 (Strength or Shadow?) Am I using the archetype in a strength or shadow way?				
Step #2 (Archetype alone or more?) Am I using the archetype in balance or alone?				

Step #3 (Archetype to bridge the gap?) What archetype story do I need to create in my thought river to create a bridge to accomplish Phase 1?				

Addendum E – Sample Stakeholder Survey Questions

Choose from the question bank below to increase stakeholder engagement and collect anonymous survey data to determine perceptions and expectations for the new leader.

- *Describe the qualities of our next leader that would make them the best fit for our organization.*
- *From your perspective, what do you believe are the most immediate challenges we face that our new leader will need to tackle?*
- *What do you believe are the two or three long-term challenges our organization will need to address in the near future?*
- *What leadership background and skills will be needed to address those challenges?*
- *What beliefs and values does our new leader need to demonstrate each day to fill our current gap?*
- *What specific capabilities and qualities will set our best-fit candidate apart from the others?*
- *What management style is preferred for the new leader?*
- *What legacy should the new leader leave at the end of their tenure?*
- *What climate (attitudes in the workplace) and culture (belief systems that drive actions) should the new leader foster in your workplace?*
- *What diversity, equity and inclusion experiences does the new leader need?*

Addendum F – Archetype Team Profile Sample and Gap Analysis Processing Questions

The table below illustrates a leadership team profile generated by the results of each of your individual leader's PMAI results. The team profile focuses on the three highest-scoring archetypes (inner allies) of each team member and the lowest-two-scoring archetypes. The completed table will provide a collective picture of your current team and a method to identify archetype gaps.

Leader Name	Archetype #1 (Highest)	Archetype #2	Archetype #3		Second Lowest Archetype	Lowest Archetype
Leader A						
Leader B						
Leader C						
Leader D						
Leader E						
Leader F						
Leader G						
VACANCY						

Generally, the three highest-scoring archetypes feel familiar to the leader, and that leader will tend to be skilled in the attributes and talents the three highest archetypes represent. These three highest archetypes provide feelings of authenticity, potential, and energy and represent what the leader is focused on and most interested in at the moment in time they completed the assessment. The two lowest-scoring archetypes are sometimes called "blind spots" and represent qualities that are a low priority for that leader or attributes that simply are not in their wheelhouse. (Blandin, K., Marr, H., Person, C., <u>PMAI</u> Manual. 2021)

Gap Analysis Questions:

1. Which archetypes are <u>not</u> represented in the collective team's Inner Allies (highest scoring)?
2. What impact might the absence of these archetypal tools have on the leadership team's ability to accomplish the organization's vision, mission, and goals?
3. Are there specific archetypal tools that you prefer the new leader (vacancy) display as strengths (in their top three)?

4. How fixed or fluid is my current team's profile? (Remember, archetypes are fluid in our lives. What we are today may not be what we are tomorrow. If your current team (as pictured above) has *blind spots*, they may not be a permanent lack of vision. As you bring on a new hire, however, this is the key moment to augment your team with someone who might display these *blind spot* archetypes

naturally.). But, if your team is *fixed* in their archetypal maturity, a new hire who can display these less preferred archetypes will increase the maturity of your team.

PMAI Manual. (2021) Blandin, K., Marr, H., Pearson, C. Center for Applications of Psychological Type, Inc.

Addendum G - Archetypal Word Bank

Archetype	Possible Archetypal Word Bank			
	NOUNS	**VERBS**	**ADJECTIVES**	**ADVERBS**
Idealist (Innocent)	Assumption, Chance, Hope, Possibility	Believe, Cheer, Hope, Pray, Promise, Rejoice	Bright, Faithful, Innocent, Heavenly, Optimistic, Positive, Ideal	Childishly, Positively, Optimistically
Realist (Orphan)	Awareness, Complaint, Problem, Reality, Safety, Security, Union, Warning	Alert, Complain, Criticize, Protect, Rescue, Save (Savior)	Alert, Apprehensive, Careful, Cautious, Concerned, Dangerous, Suspicious, Vigilant	Dangerously, Independently, Really, Safely
Caregiver	Assistance, Care, Service, Kind	Bestow, Care, Comfort, Give, Help, Provide, Serve, Share, Support, Volunteer	Caring, Fair, Helpful, Kindhearted, Neighboring, Supportive	Gratefully, Tenderly, Voluntarily
Warrior	Ability, Courage, Competition, Outcome, Performance, Skill, Task, Work	Act, Battle, Challenge, Compete, Fight, Perform, Produce, Strengthen, Succeed	Aggressive, Brave, Combative, Productive, Courageous, Successful, Victorious	Accurately, Bravely, Fast, Masterfully, Measurably, Physically, Powerfully
Seeker	Finding, Guide, Idea, Opportunity, Solution, Way	Dream, Explore, Found, Imagine, Ponder, Tour, Travel	Adventurous, Curious, Inquisitive, Wandering	Abnormally, Imaginatively, More, Wonder
Lover	Attitude, Connection, Emotion, Heart, History, Love, Passion, Value, Relationship, Tradition	Accept, Belong, Connect, Feel, Hug, Include, Pledge, Remember, Unite	Anchored, Cooperative, Devoted, Friendly, Heartfelt, Passionate	Affectionately, Before, Emotionally, Lovingly Loyally, Personally, Together
Revolutionary (Destroyer)	Examination, Quality, Responsibility, Tension	Analyze, Examine, Prevent, Question, Replace, Scrape, Trouble	Abandoned, Breakable, Concerned, Defiant, Damaged, Vacate	Appropriately, Candidly, Efficiently, Why
Creator	Building, Construct, Product, Resource	Build, Created, Fix, Invent, Replace, Repair, Improve	Authentic, Beneficial, Better, Crafty, Clever, Creative, Functional	Colorfully, Structurally, Stylishly, Visually
Ruler	Administration, Boss, Control, Method, Plan, Policy, Power, Procedure, Strategy	Command, Expect, Plan, Reign, Rule	Absolute, Authorized, Hierarchal, Obedient, Orderly, Powerful, Responsive	Chiefly, Methodically, Neatly, Officially, Rigidly
Magician	Balance, Growth, Impact, Insight, Training	Admonish, Cause, Change, Encourage, Heal, Improve, Repair, Transform	Better, Charismatic, Encouraging, Intuitive, Mindful, Prime	Acutely, Magically, Spiritually, Inwardly

Sage	Analysis, Advice, Education, Knowledge, Thought, Truth, Understanding	Analyze, Consider, Educate, Influence, Inquire, Know, Learn, Teach, Theorize	Academic, Brainy, Contemplative, Educated, Knowing, Sarcastic, Thoughtful	Intelligently, Studiously, Scientifically, Seriously, Wisely
Jester	Entertainment, Excitement, Fun, Game	Enjoy, Explain, Jest, Joke, Laugh, Play, Smile, Surprise	Amused, Cheerful, Easy, Funny, Happy, Joyous, Playful	Cheerfully, Jubilantly, Playfully, Joyously

Addendum H - 6-Minute Screening Criteria

Criteria for Analyzing Candidate 6-minute Screening Videos or Audio Submissions	
Did the candidate articulately and completely answer the structured questions you posed? Evidence:	YES or NO
Do the candidates, beliefs, values, passions, and purpose align with your organization? Are there gaps to fill? Evidence:	YES or NO
Did they highlight their qualifications and why they are your best candidate based on the job posting? Evidence:	YES or NO
What keywords and phrases are they using that give you clues to archetype strengths? Evidence:	YES or NO
Can you detect a fixed or fluid mindset with their word choice? Evidence:	FIXED or FLUID
Did they reference your organization's vision, mission and/or core values and explain how they align with them? Evidence:	YES or NO
Is the candidate using positive, professional language that is appropriate for the position you have posted? Are you hearing any slang? Evidence:	YES or NO
Did the candidate take the opportunity to showcase their personality? Evidence:	YES or NO
Do you have any inclination as to if the candidate will fill the gaps you identified? Evidence:	YES or NO
Did the candidate use all of the 6-minute time allotment? *(Quality candidates generally can fill the entire 6 minutes.)* Time: _____	YES or NO
What archetypal language did you hear? *(Reference word bank that corresponds with each archetype.)* Does the language you heard align with the archetype(s) you are seeking for this position?	YES or NO
Other Evidence:	

Addendum I – Candidate Data Organizer

CANIDATE NAME: _____

DATA & OBSERVATIONS

ENGAGE STAFF — Engage stakeholders (survey); align needs; administer PMAI assessment to existing team; conduct gap analysis on data. **1**
2 BETTER JOB POSTING — Draft new & improved job posting with additional components to attract candidates that fill gap.
6-MINUTE SCREENER — Candidates submit structured video for pre-screening prior to face-to-face meeting. Gain insights on who will fill your gap. **3**
4 NARROW & ASSESS — Narrow the candidate field and administer PMAI to candidates prior to face-to-face meeting.
PERSONAL INTERVIEW — First face-to-face meeting that includes scenario-based questions to assess alignment of answers to PMAI data. **5**
6 PERFORMANCE DEMONSTRATION — Narrowed field completes performance-based assessment.
SELECT NEW LEADER — Based on all data, select leader that is the best fit for the gap you are filling. **7**

What behavior and character traits about this candidate respond to the stakeholder survey data? What about this candidate fills a team PMAI needs/gaps:
What evidence suggests that this candidate aligns with your vision, mission, and non-negotiable core tenets and guiding principles? Does this candidate have the competencies and talents that meet your expectations? Is there a gap?
What evidence suggests that his candidate's beliefs, values, passions, and purpose align to your expectations/your organization's needs? Are there gaps to fill?
What gaps does this candidate have? Are the gaps that this candidate has coachable?
Do this candidate's responses to the scenario-based questions align with the competency and archetypal gaps you've identified? Do the candidate's answers align with their PMAI assessment?
How did the candidate score on the performance-based "job audition?" Did the audition affirm competency?
Objectively, does this candidate have gaps that are too great for the position? Are the gaps coachable and fillable?

Made in the USA
Monee, IL
01 October 2024

67026032R00096